Goodbye Late 20's

Goodbye Late 20's

GLORIA MULLONS

 www.trafford.com

North America & international
toll-free: 1 888 232 4444 (USA & Canada)
fax: 812 355 4082

Contents

On You

The past few days have been nice,
The goal stays in the moment,
I tried but accept defeat,
Mother Nature has arrived,
Mornings prior to her arrival I wake,
Mornings prior to her arrival I imagine us,
Mornings prior to her arrival I'm on you in every way,
Mother Nature has arrived,
All I want is to lie on you,
All I want is to hear your heartbeat,
All I want is to caress your stomach with my hands and mouth,
All I want is to rub your chest and feel the hair, which has permanent residence unlike me,
All I want is to be on you,
Not sexually 'cause I can't because of Mother Nature,
Being on you is what I crave,
Hungry for your space,
All I want is to be on you.

Senses

Not sure how this came to be,
Me being able to detect your highs and lows,
Perhaps spending days working on projects,
Maybe,
Perhaps having eye contact,
Perhaps it was the touches on the shoulder,
Maybe,
Perhaps it was the jokes,
Whatever it may be I'm happy to know that I can sense your highs
and lows,
Never thought this would be although I would not change it for
the world,
I finally get it,
Having a genuine concern for another person,
Learning about your highs and lows, I finally get it,
Senses,
We both get it.

Common

Our space,
Our things,
Our purpose,
Common we have the above,
Our passion to serve God,
Our passion to serve the universe,
Our person to serve the people,
Our love for music,
Our love for travel,
Our appreciation for style,
Our appetite for breakfast foods,
Our appetite for peanut butter,
Our need to be by the window on planes,
Our birthday May 19,
Most importantly our love for one another,
Common we have the above,
Not to mention our strong like for literature.

Plans

Plans are good,
Life doesn't always go according to the plan,
Plans are good,
Woke up this morning blessed and thankful,
Turned on the tube for the political dishings,
Cleaned up my face and some spaces around the house,
Made my plans for the day,
The phone rings,
Caller ID says who it is,
The phone rings again and again,

My plans were placed on hold,
Receiving news that Big Mama was not doing so well,
Managed to shower and head to the 8th floor,
Managed to explain to my 74-year-old grandmother that her
83-year-old girlfriend had suffered minor series of strokes and she
was about a mile or two away at Weiss Memorial hospital where
the two of you worked for 30-plus years,
Managed to keep my cool while explaining all the events that occurred,
Not sure if it's intuition or wisdom but you knew that something
wasn't right,
Life does not always go according to the plan.

Arrival

Grandmother and I manage to find a park on Marine drive
insisting not to go into the lot, we walk arm in arm,
Heads low to fight the cold wind and rain,
Somehow you manage to give a lesson in the structure of Weiss
Hospital and how when you started working there were only 2–4
floors,
Times have changed and the hospital has expanded significantly
there are 8-plus floors now,
It's been so long since I last visited,
Walking into the lobby,
Not sure if anyone is still here that I know,
The receptionist jumps out of her seat at the sight of you,
Oh my, where have you been?
You look so good,
Joy, love, excitement,
Tell me this,
How is she?
Well, if I didn't know her before I wouldn't have recognized her today,
It doesn't look good.

ICU

The doors to the 2nd-floor elevator opened,
Arrows point to the left for intensive care unit,
My body is in a daze it seems,
The hallway is quiet a visitor confirms the right direction for ICU,
At the reception areas a longtime friend recognizes you; in fact
people come in from all over the hospital to say hello to Grandma,
My body snaps back into reality,
She's in room #4,
No matter what they say you can never prepare for the emotions
you feel when seeing a love one in pain,
As humans we have a need to heal and solve,
Today I learned an important lesson,
As humans we cannot do it all,
Immediately Grandmother walked to her friends bedside,
My eyes full of tears that could not drop,
Grandmother rubbed her hands and called her name,
The left side of her body responded while the right side remained
still,
Her eyes rolled from the left then right,
No words ever came because they couldn't,
She was in a different ICU.

I'm Sorry

I'm sorry,
From the bottom of my heart,
I understand that it was not easy visiting your mother during her last days on earth,
I'm sorry for pushing you to visit,
I now know that watching a loved one in a facility is not an easy task,
I now know that it takes a lot out of a person to sit in a room for hours and watch a loved one moan and remain quiet,
While you watch helplessly,
I felt the pain because I saw it in Grandmother's good girlfriend eyes,
As I entered the room, her eyes followed me; I manage to sit on the window sill where I was out of view,
Grandmother continued to rub her hands and fix her gown while tucking the blanket underneath her to ensure warmth,
My thoughts immediately went to you,
I wondered if you felt the same way I did about watching your loved one and not being able to do anything,
I'm sorry,
Please know my intentions were good,
Somehow I felt if I was forceful and persistent,
That would make you see how important visiting consistently especially during difficult times,
I pushed to hard,
Not knowing what you were up against,
I take it all back,
Well, at least some of it,
Many times you shared about the visits never thought they were difficult,
I wish you could have had someone with you each day to comfort You after or during your visits,
I know how strong you are but who will you let be strong for you,
Honestly I know we make a good team.

You Are

My sunshine,
My passion for change,
My sunshine,
My breath of fresh air on a stuffy day,
My melody to life,
My flavor of love,
My desire,
You are all that I want,
You are the dream I want to live,
You are the man for me,
You are,
You are simply you.

I Can't

Never before have I been stalled to react,
I can't be mad at you,
Never before have I been so penetrated that I hardly recognize my
stubbornness or lack their of,
I can't be mad at you for no amount of time,
Never has someone made me loose my toughness,
I can't believe I've transformed,
Never would I have thought you'd have such a deep impact on my
day-to-day feelings,
Now there have been times you have made my blood boil but it
eventually cools down and I find myself wanting to kiss your face,
I can't believe that I want you even more when we have
misunderstandings or disagreements,
Never do my feelings change about you,
I can believe that we we'll have a good time.

Knock-Knock

To the best of my knowledge I've shared,
It was not easy at first,
I know we have no title,
I'm single so are you,
I wonder if you always shared with me,
You're holding back,
I know what happened during overseas travel,
My heart ached for you,
Gosh, I feel so gullible,
Gosh, I feel so naive,
Yes, you hurt yourself,
You caused the pain,
My heart aches for you,
I've done nothing but offer sympathies,
Yes, I understand your pain is real,
Will you ever reveal the truth,
Acceptance is my pledge,
I pray that God will heal,
Your mind, spirit, and soul.

Little Play

The beginning of a new day brings about endless opportunities,
So far things are quiet except for the usual events on Monday,
Somehow our paths cross,
Somehow I walked passed your office,
Situated behind your desk,
So focused on your screen,
We make eye contact,
We smile,
You extend your tongue,
You extend your tongue and curl the tip,
You have me thinking,
You have me licky-licky,
You have me thinking what would it feel like to taste your tongue;
it's flexible,
Wonder if you enjoy traveling to the deep forest,
Licky-licky,
I can't wait.

Morning Chitchat

Love it when we chitchat,
Sometimes it playful,
Well, most of the time it's playful,
Today was unusual,
Chitchat started off with smiles and laughter,
Escalated to silence and a statement,
Maybe it was my fault I challenged you,
The challenge was opposed as it should have been,
Yes, I'm aware that you can do and be anything you want,
Sorry, baby, for ruffling your position,
You say you were being factious,
I took you seriously,
Sorry, baby,
I could not communicate what I really meant,
You are such a sharp dresser from head to toe, I could not imagine
you not having feet, well, at least that was my thoughts, It was not
meant to make
you feel any differently.

Gift

The day started off blurry,
Upon hearing your voice,
Positive energy filled the room,
The day brought about many things, coordinated dinner with five
people,
Received phone calls and text of holiday well wishes and Happy
New Year,
All my thoughts are about you,
All I want is to see and touch you,
All I can think about during dinner is getting to where you are,
All I know is that when dinner ended, I was overjoyed to share
moments with my family,
Finally make it to you, dressed casually; you are looking good,
We exchanged gifts,
Have nice conversation,
All I want has been granted seeing you,
We part,
We kiss good-bye our first on the lips,
We kiss for a nice time,
It's sweet in every way.

Afterglow

No matter what I do I can't erase the thought of our first kiss,
I wanted it to happen,
I wasn't nervous, neither were you,
We exchanged gifts; I thanked you with a kiss on the cheek for
your gift,
We sat close,
When you unwrapped my gift, you beamed and said thank you,
You leaned over to thank me, so did I,
Our lips met,
You were in control kissing my top lip,
You were in control kissing and sucking my bottom lip,
Moaning in pleasure as we kissed,
You said something about all my lips tasting as good,
I'm sure you will find out,
The kiss was soft and sweet, your hand on my chin

Home

The evening has set in,
The temperature is below 30 degrees.
The sounds of engines roar on Lake Shore Drive,
The streetlights illuminate the pavement,
I'm at home,
There's a small garden-like property located next to building,
Many years ago Grandpa planted a tree,
The tree is tall and strong,
The holiday season has brought bright lights to the trees,
Glancing out the window at Grandpa's tree is proof of the simple things in life,
Amazing what human life can do,
Trees are such a vibrant reflection of God's work,
Each day I look at tree, I'm reminded of the soul of Grandpa,
Grandma confided in me that indeed Grandpa planted this tree a long time ago, maybe the 60s, 70s or 80s,
I'm at home.

It's Not Easy

Each day I've tried to go about regular activity,
It's not easy,
Last heard from you on Thursday evening,
It's not easy,
Little concerned when I didn't receive a call Friday morning,
It's not easy,
Later I thought you must have been busy with getting ready for
your trip,
I phoned,
Sent a text,
No response,
Saturday came and went I pray that you are okay,
It's not easy,
Late Saturday evening I send e-mail.
No response,
I'm worried about you, I must admit,
It's not easy not hearing from you,
Sunday comes; I pray that all is well with you,
All sorts of thoughts enter my mind and I dismiss those thoughts,
Immediately I remember the purpose of your trip,
It's not easy,
Your army buddy lost his son,
It's not easy,
A true friend you are to be with him,
It's not easy,
It's only been a few months since you parted from your mom,
It's not easy, I pray that God watches over your friend and his
entire family through this ordeal,
I pray that you are strong and healthy,
It's not easy to be away from you, but life calls for such activity,
It's not easy but such event is a reminder that we are alive and
indeed in the moment.

New Year's Morning

The day started with a golf lesson,
Face drenched like rains,
Body indeed got tested,
Felt like Gloria Gaynor song I will survive,
Entering the elements sweat maintained,
Felt the workout,
Felt proud,
Stomach in knots,
We speak,
Set a date if I may say so,
Slipped on a casual dress and boots,
The beginning of a new day brings about all sorts of opportunities,
This day we met at the pancake house,
Sandwiched between two existing customers,
We place our orders,
Look directly at one another for the most part,
Catching up on politics, golf, work,
The beginning of a new day brings about all sorts of opportunities.

New Year's Evening

24 hours before New Year's Eve,
I propose we hang out,
The timing was off,
Things needed to be fixed at your place,
I propose we hang out,
We shared breakfast; it was nice,
You talked through the pain,
We walked to our vehicles,
We hugged,
You giving me a special pat on the butt,
Your car was next to mine on a patch of ice,
I commented that you like to climb on things,
You say I want you to climb on me,
I say yes, I do,
We part,
Smiling from the inside because of you,
Five hours later,
I receive a text,
You ask if I want to get together,
Yes, I reply,
You arrive,
Looking delicious,
I take your coat and hat,
Place the champagne on the table,
We hug,
We kiss,

Get the glasses ready for the toast to New Year's,
Happy New Year's,
We toast,
We kiss,
We toast,
Look at one another,
We move to the couch,
Talk and channel surf,
This feels good,
Still can't believe you are here with me,
We spent the whole day together practically at least,
We prepare for bed,
Another treat being under the same roof as you,
Feels magical,
We wake,
Feels nice to see you,
We shower,
We dress,
We talk,
We channel surf,
We lie side by side,
We eat take out,
We lie side by side,
The evening is upon us,
We cuddle, we kiss, you leave.

Be Cool

You are not your best,
Be cool,
You are not your best,
Reaching out to you is normal in the evening,
You are not well you share,
Heart aches for you,
Be cool, you tell me,
Be cool with the texts,
Okay, I say and God bless you,
I'm worried deeply about you but I will give you what you asked
for love G.

Need to Fix Things

The afternoon is upon us,
Attempts to reach you are unsuccessful,
Wondering how you are feeling,
You don't want to talk about your pain,
You are upset; I can sense in your voice,
Not sure if there is anything I can do but be here for you,
Your environment has not been aired or cleaned,
I sense your tension when we talk,
We talk briefly,
Nice to hear your voice,
Just wanted to say hi,
Afraid to ask how you are because you don't want to talk about
how you feel,
That's all you wanted you say,
Yes,
I'm going over some golf drills,
Okay.

No Talking

When we don't talk I still think of you,
Life dish challenges,
As the receivers we deal,
Together we know anything can be achieved,
There are things only you can fix,
I'm here for you,
When it feels like you are shutting me out I breathe and release
such a thought,
I'm here for you,
When we don't talk I still think of you.

Miss you

Three nightfalls have passed,
Three sunrises,
Off to the nation's capital you are,
A historic moment we are in,
Miss you, I do,
Nightfalls are filled with moments we've shared,
Sunrises are drenched in smiles we've shared,
Miss you, I do,
No correspondence,
Hoping you are well,
Pray for you each night,
Miss you, I do,
Your eyes,
Your touch,
Your company,
Miss you, I do.

Oops! Jill Biden

The day before presidential inauguration, *Oprah* is broadcasting
live from the Kennedy Center in Washington, DC,
Millions are tuned in,
Ashton and Demi are the first guests explaining their efforts for
public service pledge,
Amazing to see the level of involvement by all citizens of this
country,
The next guests, Joe and Jill Biden,
The crowd roars,
The topic goes to the role of Joe Biden,
Jill chimes in and makes a boo-boo,
Joe was offered secretary of state and vice president,
The audience is quiet,
Awkward moment maybe,
Truthful moment priceless.

The Walnut Room

The former vice president Al Gore is in town,
Much talk about how he will be the best act out of the series of speakers,
A ticket you have to attend the affair,
Off to dinner we go,
I'm glad just to be with you,
Off to the Walnut Room we go,
The room is lovely,
The view of State Street landscape is breathtaking,
We talk about work-related events,
The highs and lows,
Your introduction to "Green industry" started in Texas, Route 35,
which can be accessed in Iowa and other major cities,
There was a mutual understanding; the change is in the midst,
The company is pleasant,
Dinner is good,
We talk more about living arrangements, and tenant rights,
My living arrangements are ideal; I don't need more,
After being serious, we tease,
Teasing mellows the moment,
Teasing allows us to be free and enjoy the essence of life,
We maintain eye contact throughout the evening,
Dinner is delicious tilapia for me, meatballs for you,
Dessert we share, chocolate cheesecake, two forks, I tease about licking your fork,
The evening comes to an end,
We walk to State Street,

You go to the Chicago Theater and I to bus stop,
We pause and kiss publicly sweet,
We pause and kiss mouth to mouth, feels good,
As I board the bus, I can't help but to think about how much you
miss your mom and doing things that she enjoyed,
Please know that it's natural to feel the way you do; however,
remember all the precious moments you had while she was alive—
keep those moments alive and she will always remain in your
heart—I love how you show your emotions.

Speeding

The day is beautiful,
I drop my honey by the office,
Head to computer lab to modify résumé for a job fair at Illinois
Institute of Technology,
So far the day is going okay,
On my way home I decide to look for a copy center to print résumé,
No luck,
I decide to go home because I'm hungry and it's lunchtime,
The property manager agrees to print my résumé,
I head to my place and eat a tuna sandwich heated,
Its 1pm,
I'm feeling irritated and have a headache,
My mind begins to wonder about driving or public transportation
or do I need to go,
I pull it together after talking to my honey,
I decide to get cleaned up and head out to 314 S. Federal Street,
Greeted by the warmth of sun,
Lake Shore Drive is beautiful,
Upon exiting 31st Street there's a black 4-door Charger behind me,
The car barely swipes my front right lights trying to get in front of me,
I let them go,
A car full of 3-4 young girls driving too fast and not paying
attention was my observation,
After driving further on 31st the black Dodge speeds past me and
through the light,
I pause,

Noticing a gray ford focus in the path of this speeding car while
Chicago's finest speeds by in pursuit of what I don't know,
This is bad,
This scene could be out of a movie,
The speeding black car smashes into the silver Ford Focus with a
side impact; glass shatters everywhere,
The girls jump out of the car,
1 girl falls to the ground,
The police pull up,
Not sure how the driver is doing in the silver Ford Focus,
Everyone driving stops,
I pull over,
Nerves are a mess,
I go home.

Change

My biggest challenge,
Struggled since I was a young girl,
Or did I?
My biggest challenge is accepting the change I've asked for,
My biggest challenge is knowing that good exists in the change,
I have weak moments,
The cravings,
Thinking no one notices my behavior,
No longer can I hide,
No longer can I add miles and trails of unsavory behavior,
Food is for nutrition and not console or comfort let alone feeling
a void,
From this day forward,
My biggest challenge is to accept change.

Breathe

Lately,
Feeling stuck,
Not in a physical sense,
Lately the universe has positioned me for all that I've asked for,
Lately I've realized that everything I've ever wanted has been provided to me,
Lately I've changed my mental preferences toward food,
Lately I've learned that animals go through a lot just to arrive in local stores,
Lately I've discovered that there's a connection with animals,
Lately I've learned to breathe; I realize that's a job for the individual,
Each day is a pleasurable exhale.

Estrogen

Here we go,
Seems familiar,
A familiar not welcome,
Today I learned some things about estrogen,
Estrogen fluctuates,
Particularly around a menstrual cycle due to some things,
Meat,
Fat,
Saturated or saturation,
You name it and it has a cause on a woman's body ... mood swings,
In order for women to avoid fluctuation, we must have a high fiber
diet ... beans and veggies,
No meat,
No fat,
No saturated fat,
A plant-based diet is strongly recommended,
I continue to struggle with making the right decision,
I've sampled a plant-based diet but lose sight of the purpose,
No longer will I make excuses,
I will live with a purpose.

Blood Clots

Been meaning to return your call last week,
I call you back,
You're at the hospital in emergency room,
His condition has shifted,
Blood clots are in his lungs,
At this moment you are with doctors talking about options for
resuscitation,
Your voice is trembling,
I feel your pain,
I indicate I will call you back,
Drop to my knees,
Pray to God to remove the clots,
Strengthen him all over,
Cover his body in your godly greatness,
Guard him,
Watch over the entire family,
Give them the strength and courage,
He will pull through,
He is a fighter,
God, keep and soothe your family,
May 7,
Two days have passed,
He has passed and now rest with your mother.

Flavor

The day started usual,
Somewhat tired,
Mother Nature is on her way,
And I walked on the lakefront yesterday,
Many people out enjoying the beautiful day,
As I thanked God for opening my eyes off to the bathroom I go,
New Sensodyne foaming toothpaste is awesome,
My thoughts drift to you,
We text,
Complications arise with your phone,
We talk it out,
You end up asking me to do exactly what you ask,
I listen and comply, sensing that you are in no mood to indulge in
problem-solving skills,
I listen and get specific instructions,
Conversation end and I do as you ask,
I text you confirmation of task and phone you,
Immediately you say that you love me,
I say I love you too,
We end conversation,
Head to the kitchen and rinse grapes and cherries, placed in
refrigerator for the week,
Get cleaned up.

Free write

Good morning, universe and God. My eyes are open and my body is aching, perhaps a sign that that Mother Nature is on her way. My scarf is still on from last night; however, I can feel the tightness around the crown of my head, or shall I say, the outside area. My retainers are both in my mouth not shockingly because one evening they both came out and that freaked me out. As I sit on the magic toilet bowl; surely this is something different for me, not so bad. I'm just writing freestyle, doing something different and living in the moment. Tried my best not to focus on previous thoughts as I lay in the bed before I made it to the bathroom. Thoughts were all over the place as they usually are once I open my eyes. It also feels good that I did not pick up my iPhone immediately before I washed my face and brushed my teeth. Today, I will clean up first before I do pick up the gadget.

News

Life is precious,
Tomorrow is not promised,
These sayings are true,
As I sit up alert on this Thursday morning,
Learning of the murder of my cousin,
Killed,
On the west side,
Shot several times,
It's 2:00 a.m. in the morning,
The news came over the phone,
The voice of my aunt,
Calm,
Thought I was dreaming,
Surely I was,
Grandma came down around midnight,
We talked until we could no more,
I lie across the bed,
30 minutes later the house phone rings,
and it's an Aunt with this news
officially,
Although I think it was Grandma who sensed this first,
The second oldest grandchild
of the kids gone on to that special place.

Homecoming

A sweet homecoming,
Sealed with a warm embrace,
Bodies blended,
Eyes and spirits exchanging the purity of the moment.

Arrangements

It's the wee hours of the morning,
Arrived at home,
Exhausted from making selections,
Selections of photos and words,
The day's events,
Hugs,
Tears,
Many phone calls,
All surrounding cousin,
Managed to make it to the gym,
Sweat,
Run some errands,
Pick up my honey,
On and on,
Got a call from David but he doesn't show.

July

Up until a little after 1:00 a.m.,
Simmering in the heat of ecstasy,
The cold breeze from the AC further relaxes our bodies,
The alarm sounds,
We cuddle,
Embracing the bareness,
Cheek to cheek,
The temperature of the day fills the 2-bedroom apartment,
A quick change of the sheets,
Then a cool soapy shower,
Followed by packing shirts and suits for cleaners,
It's hot out,
Thank God for another day,
Upon making it home plans are made to visit body at A. A. Rayner
Funeral Home,
Grandma and I go,
Somehow I thought I'd be okay,
I'm not; I cry upon seeing face from entrance of door,
He looks as though sleep is the only concern,
Grandma holds me tight,
I cry until it's out,
A senseless murder,

Uncle arrives,
He falls to his knees and pray while hands rest on casket,
We sit,
More visitors arrive,
We leave,
Head begins to pound,
Make it home,
Have dinner at a mom-and-pop Mexican restaurant,
Waiting for Sears service man to arrive to fix AC unit,
It's 90 degrees,
No AC growing up, why is this any different?
Sears serviceman given incorrect information to service AC unit,
Another hot night,
More phone calls and text messages,
I've decided to not appear at funeral,
I ask God to give me what I need during this time as I'm confused,
I have to consider my safety,
You understand,
My fear is that I have this elephant on my shoulder,
I have no idea the specifics of why you were murdered; only God knows,
Rest in peace.

Books Inks 2nd Annual Community Festival

Not much rest before the first book signing,
Not much rest after the book signing,
Excited about the previous day's events,
So much so I'm up writing because my body will not let me rest just yet,
I've had pizza two days in a row so my allergies have slightly flared up,
Eyes are somewhat itchy but I recognize my fault,
I sit and write listening to the AC and cars on Lake Shore Drive,
Thoughts of the book fest float in my mind,
Very appreciative for all who attended,
A former coworker who is a writer,
A former chairperson of a prestigious organization,
A mentor who believed that I had the gift for speaking,
Two good friends indeed,
Another former colleague who helped me pack up,
Two phone calls received about attending but after 7:30 p.m. I called it quits,

Grandma is with me every step of the way,
Grandma, my blessing,
Grandma, we have come along way,
Grandma took me in after Mother passed in 1999,
Grandma, I'm so glad you are here sharing this moment with me,
Dear God, I thank you for all of your blessings for I am your student,
Dear God, continue to guide me and do as you see fit, Heavenly
Father, for I am yours,
Dear God, thank you for instilling in me hope and dreams,
Dear God, thank you; I know it's not enough for all that you do but
please know my heart is embedded in your existence,
Dear God, continue to guide me in your will,
Dear God, I love you and thank you.

Mothers Birthday

I'm up,
Feeling okay,
Just finished dinner,
Greens,
Turkey necks,
Tomatoes and peppers,
Hot water corn bread,
I first prayed to the beloved animal that afforded such a meal,
I prayed that the spirit be released to God and I meant it,
The movie *Avatar* brought this to my attention,
To give thanks to the animal humankind brother/sister,
As we all are connected,
I truly believe that,
Watched the soaps,
Mo'Nique Show and Wendy Williams,
Ended the evening with *Sex and the City* on TBS,
Today is Mother's birthday,
For the first time in many years I feel okay,
I will always love my Mother and cherish all memories,
I text Big Brother to see how he's doing,
Overall so-so,
Was the message conveyed over the phone,
Having some car trouble,
I tell him to call me if he needs me,
God, protect him.

More on Mom

Another day,
It's taken some time to arrive at,
Another day,
Today,
The day,
September 2,
The birth of my mother,
Yes,
Today is another day,
A day that God has granted all on earth to live,
I rise before 9:00 a.m.,
Greeted by rain,
A day of studying covers the calendar,
Off I go to Truman City College,
The environment is different,
Different after attending an HBCU in North Carolina,
Then transferring to the small town of Carlinville,
Can't forget about living in DC for a semester,
Final destination, University of Ill at Chicago for graduate school,
Yes, all these experiences make attending a city college different,
or does it?
All is well with the computer courses in that I'm very eager to
learn about the new operating systems and programs in the word
or world,
Coupled with writing a book I feel reborn.

This Feels Good

Lips upon your skin,
Discovering the sweet spot of your harvest,
Tears of joy escape me as we journey through the fields of
lovemaking,
Lips upon your skin kissing,
Sucking,
Nibbling,
Becoming full from your love,
Ego doesn't want me to give feedback,
Ego, I cannot listen to you,
I tell my lover,
You make me feel great,
This feels good, baby,
Moans escape me like breathing,
Naturally,
Freely,
Yes,
My lips upon your skin,
Your lips upon my skin,
As we tend to the bodies,
By giving and receiving,
I love you, love.

Professor Nanetti

The sound of cars I hear along Lake Shore Drive,
The lake breeze cools my home,
Tree leaves move slightly from the wind,
It is Thursday morning US time,
Perhaps you are currently in flight or have already arrived a day
or two in advance, on this day,
The university pays tribute to your many years of service,
On this day I reflect on my exposure to you,
Five years ago I sat on the first row of your Introduction to
Planning or History of Planning course,
Eager about the world of planning,
You begin lecturing,
Covering events, places, and people,
A month or two pass,
And the first paper is due,
Not only am I a student,
A full-time government employee for an elected official,
The proper amount of time I did not give to the first paper,
And as such you returned to me,
To do over,
You can do better than this,

I'll admit I'd thrown something together,
Reality set in,
Revisiting the paper on Chicago's Black Belt or Greenbelt (south side of Chicago) required real research and focus,
Eventually the paper was resubmitted and I knew that I could not behave in such a manner again as a graduate student,
I often wondered,
Perhaps I shouldn't have,
As to what you saw in me to know I could do better,
Looking back on the experience,
Allows me to appreciate your role as a professor,
A true concern you expressed for my performance,
I've had a many teachers and professors,
By far you have been the best and not just in an academic sense,
Your spirit,
And concern are genuine,
Over the years I've grown personally and professionally,
Because of you,
Thank you, Professor Nanetti,
May you enjoy the next part of your journey on earth.

City College

City college,
Feels like an out-of-body experience,
Perhaps I've been spoiled by taking college courses in high school,
By attending a four year college,
By going to graduate school,
City college, a different experience indeed,
The location of school in a gentrifying area,
All walks of life
are seen,
Drug users,
Sellers,
Professionals,
Mental patients,
Teenagers,
You name it, and like most cities and parts of town, it exists,
I feel grateful for all that I have in my life,
This point in my life brings me back to the importance of the basics,
Attending classes on time,
Doing the required readings,
Being involved in class,

Labtime

Wednesday evening,
Enter the lab for computer information systems (CIS 116)
Always eager for the lecture by Professor T,
Loving a minority instructor,
He may be Cambodian or Filipino; I will find out,
I've learned much in four weeks of class,
Such as knowing the difference between an operating system and
a application,
Such as knowing the importance of file management,
Such as protecting your computer with antivirus software and
other programs,
All this and more,
So,
Why is it that my classmates,
Not all classmates,
But some,
Moan and groan about the homework assignments and in class
handouts,
The moaning and groaning come from the white males,
There are at least 22 or 32 students,
Out of the 22–32,
3 are black males,

3 black women,
1 Indian,
2 Hispanics,
The bulk of the class is male,
The majority at times cry like babies; at times I want to give them
a pacifier,
Clearly the professor has earned his right to teach,
We as students are present to learn,
The professor often reminds us that he is here to help students,
I value that comment,
On this evening one student has the nerve to tell the professor
that the assignments seem to be busywork and repetitive,
Oh my,
God, please help those that are lost,
God, reveal everyone's purpose so they will not continue to be
blinded by the ego.

Foreign Service

Just returning home after attending a Foreign Service prep session,
Specifically for the written exam,
The previous ambassador in residence never got back to me about
prep session in August,
I guess I saw this as a sign,
Not sure if the sign was positive or negative,
Fast-forward two days before the exam,
I e-mail ambassador in residence,
Received auto response from e-mail,
Position has been vacated,
News is given about new diplomat in residence,
I find out that the prep session is today,
I get ready,
Grandmother comes down,
We leave the house going separate ways,
Call me when you get back so we can figure out what's for dinner,
The prep sessions begin a little after 3:00 p.m.,
There are four attendees, including myself,
A white male contractor and IT company owner,
A DePaul college junior,
Both have lived in Budapest, Hungary,
A Russian lady who speaks 2–3 other languages,
And me,
We go around and introduce ourselves,
Shortly after the presentation begins by the diplomat in residence,

Who's not technologically savvy,
A round woman,
A bob hairdo,
Pleasant,
Blue eyes,
Has lived in Sierra, Mexico, and several other places,
Has worked about 20 years for the State Department,
Many stories are shared about her various tours,
I think to God, should I be doing this,
Much info is learned about the test,
2 ½ hours,
Electronic,
No notes,
Know the 13 qualifications,
Know the capital of countries,
Practice having a conversation for 30 minutes about a topic that is
unknown to you,
50,000 people take exam annually,
Only 2,000–3,000 get in,
This is a hard exam,
A combination of the LSAT, GRE, and GMAT,
God, is this for me,
Help me,
More information given about preparation,
My anxiety or concern level rises somewhat,
Just like with the LSAT,

Is history repeating itself? Should I even be doing this,
Read real news,
CNN,
BBC,
The Economist,
Forgot about Fox; that's not news,
The session ends,
Are there any questions,
Gloria, are you ready,
Nope,
Or perhaps I am,
Mentally taking this test without preparation would probably be the best opportunity for me if I follow my guts,
What do I have to lose,
If I take it, at least I'll know if I have what it takes,
If I don't take it, will I worry about what could have been,
If I take it and don't do well, do I invest the time and energy into something that I'm not passionate about,
The previous evening I stayed up researching child care nationally with respect to that group being a target population in my business plan,
This gets me passionate about work.

A Prayer

Dear God, I need you,
For only you know my soul,
Dear God, I come to you with a heavy heart at my own doing,
Dear God, please touch me as you know I'm in need,
For only you, God, can set me straight,
My mind is rattled,
My heart beating fast,
Tears,
Fill my eyes for I am troubled over a decision,
One in particular on this day,
Dear God, I release to you my burden of the Foreign Service office exam,
I release the burden,
The unknown,
All I release in your hands, trusting that you will lead the way,
Dear God, please speak to me as you do,
I will listen,
Dear God, I love you and you're first always in my life.

Listen

Will you listen to me,
And not analyze,
Will you let me share my concerns and not diagnose the problem,
As I'm already aware of the problem,
Will you just listen,
I know you care,
I love you for caring,
Will you allow me to vent,
Surely you read between the lines better than I,
That's an awesome quality to have,
I on the other hand go about things differently,
My guts have always led me in the right path with God's intervention,
Will you listen to me.

Bedtime

The temperature has dropped to 45,
I've brushed my teeth,
Popped in my retainers,
Ready for bed,
It's a little after 1:00 a.m.,
Love and basketball is on BET, a sweet story,
My hands are sore from CIS 116,
Three assignments, I enjoy this kind of work, documenting all my steps,
Surely I will offer a service for learning computer operating systems,
Didn't speak to my honey,
Tried to call; perhaps he's asleep indeed,
The sounds of cars fill my house,
I need to go to sleep,
Sears repair service coming between 8:00 a.m. and 12:00 p.m.,
7 months have passed,
Still looking for work to satisfy employment security requirements,
It's true what they say about work,
Hard to find work,
I've asked God to reveal and guide my path,
PS: while visiting Grandma and Andy, I slid on the hallway rug and fell, I could only laugh at myself.

I'm Up

I'm up,
Listening to the NBA wrap up this evening,
Double header,
LA vs. Houston,
Boston vs. Houston,
Finished homework #6 for CIA 116,
Got confused about microprocessors; somehow I've managed to
compile a summary,
Reading articles for class is extra credit,
Surely I enjoy this,
My body still aches after walking to the post office on Monday,
I'm up at 12:55 a.m.,
Getting ready for bed.

Choices

Dear God,
Grant me the ability to make the right choice,
You have loaded me up with all the proper data,
Continue to stand by me and help me,
At times I revert to old ways, knowing nothing new will surface,
Making new choices is my destiny.

Snuggling

A new day,
My eyes open,
The covers are over us,
Your arms,
Warm,
Wrapped around me,
This feels good,
Safe,
Secure,
A new day,
Has brought about a sense of contentment,
Your arms,
I cannot forget,
A new day and it is beautiful with you.

Plans

It's the 1st day of *For Colored Girls* movie,
The plan for Grandma and I catch the 1:00 p.m. show,
We make it,
The film is magnificent,
It's 3:25 p.m. when we get out,
The sky is cloudy,
At 5:00 p.m. I'm to pick up my honey,
No do,
The plans change,
Andy and Mickey want to go out,
I'd plan for my honey to meet Mickey,
No such luck,
Honey will go home,
Plans don't always work out,
My evening will not be spent with honey,
Test on Monday,
Need to study,
My plan at first seemed to work,
But in the end it did not,
There is always tomorrow,
God, work with me.

Doubt

Each month,
Like the hand ticking on clock,
I have doubt about what I'm doing in my life,
Tears fill my eyes,
As I sit at home,
I have doubt,
Doubt of many things,
Movies,
Life,
And people in general can drive my thoughts wild,
But why,
Every suspicion I've had we've discussed,
So why do I end up at this place repeatedly,
The doubt I have is my ego working overtime,
God, please help me,
God, take me in your warmth and wash me of these ill thoughts.

It Happened Again

At times I just don't know what to do,
Most days I feel like I'm doing okay with this balancing act,
Until I learn of something,
And it feels like elephants are standing on my shoulders,
Aging is serious,
Much I don't know,
But learning slowly,
Missy, don't be mad at your grandma,
I feel so helpless,
Whom can I talk to,
Will she feel betrayed,
I'm worried,
We talk about a plan,
Been here before,
Missy, don't be mad at your grandma,
God, please tell me what to do.

Lawndale

Dear God,
Yesterday was a true blessing,
Got return call from company about job,
Got a return call about an interview for a facilitator position,
You have opened the door for me,
I thank you humbly,
Dear God, please continue to guide me on this newfound journey,
Working with kids,
An after-school program,
Working with kids we share logistics . . . North Lawndale,
I'm a product of the community,
Thank you, God,
Never did I doubt or not believe,
Keep all those involved and all on the planet safe,
Thank you, God, for showing me the way; I will continue to follow
and lead as you direct.

Double Dose

After receiving word about a temporary job,
Off to the doctor I go,
Working with kids require a TB test,
In my mind,
I'm thankful to God for this opportunity to work even if it's
temporary and part-time,
I am open for whatever path God will lead me on,
Once I arrive at the docs office I chitchat with the docs assistant,
The Doctor is ready for me,
First shot TB,
Next shot,
Damn, should I have gotten both?
I can handle this,
It was Thursday when I got those shots,
Three days have passed,
I have had a bumpy ride,
Friday, morning body ached, especially my arms,
Saturday, I felt delirious, so I slept,
Sunday much better,
Still feel some aches and I've sneezed a few times,
I'm up watching a reality show

GLORIA MULLONS

Walking

This day begins with rain,
I smile,
This day brings extra morning hours underneath the covers,
I smile because relaxation covers me,
This day plays smoothly,
Oh, how I love the rain,
No control over the rain,
I head outdoors, no umbrella wanting to dissolve in the drops,
I stop by the bakery for muffins,
A nap finds me but not for long,
The time arrives for my evening class,
Should I go?
Yes, of course, there's an Access exam,
I hail a cab,
Watching the rain pour down on the ground and windows,
I love the rain,
The cab arrives at school,
Puddles of water everywhere,
I love the rain against my face,
Upon entering the campus building, my pants and coat are wet,
So much love I receive on this day,
I can't say yes to everyone but I can always say yes to rain.

Snippets about Dad

As the city sleeps,
I prepare to wash my hair,
The rain has cleansed the streets and nourished the plants, crops,
and other things that require rain,
I'm reminded of my father on this day,
Although I don't remember him,
This day of Thanksgiving,
This day of Christmas,
Were his favorite holidays,
Grandmother shares this news with me each year and I often feel
closer to my father because of this,
I know it may seem odd but it helps me, build good thoughts about
my father,
Eager and excited I am to know my father enjoyed this time
of year,
I feel so blessed to be present with my grandmother as she shares
stories about the delicious meals she prepared and how my father
would dress up and enjoy dinner,
The light in Grandmother's eyes as she shares is truly memorable.

Bumps

I awake to a kiss,
From your lips,
My eyes still close,
Your touch so soft,
My body wakens slowly,
You leave the room,
I feel a sweet sensation,
Surely my body is calling for you,
The morning is open for whatever we desire,
On this day I'm feeling so sexy and ready, yet I must pause,
No, say it ain't so,
Mother Nature arrives,
With a smooth entrance,
Feel my heart with such love and excitement,
I will show you my love in a different way on this day,
We go out for brunch,
The day is sunny,
We are greeted by two church women, one who touches my arm as
she says good afternoon,
The evening arrives,
Home I go,

Dinner with the grandparents,
Grandpa's legs hurt him so,
So much so that Grandma and I hold on to his arms,
We get to the car,
Catch up on the week's events,
The restaurant is busy,
Upon leaving,
Grandpa walks slower and slower,
Getting to the apartment is a slow pace but we are patient,
I am so blessed for my grandparents,
The pain Grandpa Andy feels hurt; I will continue to do what I'm
supposed to do as a granddaughter,
We walk,
Your arm enclosed in mine,
Tears are in your eyes,
Curse words fill the hall in a low tone,
I tell you to take your time and that everything will be okay,
Your pain is real,
God, please help everyone on this earth that has pain in their
body, heart, soul,
Heal all and guide all

Cuddling

Two bodies,
Your hand behind mine,
Our arms intertwined,
Our bodies molded for the cold night,
My feet next to yours,
Warming them.

Group Interview

On my way to an interview,
In my old community,
Lawndale,
Joy I feel,
Never participated in a group interview,
Fun! Fun!
As my nephew would say,
A total of 10–12 women in the room,
We answer questions,
What's your experience with kids,
What's your experience with computers,
Define professionalism,
On and on,
The end of the interview is near,
Not so bad at all this process,
Off I go to the north side,
Grandmother is ready to take Andy to the doctor around 1:00 p.m.,
Before they I arrive home, phone rings; it's the executive director,
Ms. Mullons, I don't know what you did, but the principal and vice
president want you for an interview for the program coordinator
position,
Sure, I say,
Can you come back tomorrow?
Yes, okay.
Beaming rest of way home,

Feeling so blessed about this news,
Thank you, God,
I pick up the grandparents,
Off we go,
Sheridan and Diversey,
We arrive in front office,
Relief will come soon for Andy,
Two cortisone shots,
These past few weeks have been painful for Andy,
The pain got to him so much so that he wanted to see his
ortho doc,
By the time I enter the waiting room after parking the car,
They are finished,
Doc gave Andy prescription for pain,
He looks like a new person,
The shots burn,
But relief comes,
We hope to try acupuncture one day,
I dream of us all leaving dairy and meat alone for our health,
Working on it slowly,
Thank you, God, for giving me the time to do what you wish for
me to do, serve,
In a human sense.

Middle School

Up by 7:00 a.m.,
Out by 8:15 a.m.,
Lots of traffic,
Trucks backing into parking lots,
Blocking the streets,
What can you do?
Nothing,
Be patient,
While waiting in the office for my 9:00 a.m. appointment with the principal,
A fight occurs or is in the making,
The students are brought to the office; one sits,
The other refuses,
Security is on standby,
Shortly after situation occurs,
A student just walks out the room with no note,
The teacher arrives in the office,
He doesn't need a parent's phone call,
He needs to sit down and learn,
Call me when he talks with the principal,
Did I forget the little boy who was sitting in the office when I arrived; not sure what his story is,

Lots going on before 10:00 a.m.,
There is so much going on with people in general,
Who knows what made these kids so feisty this morning,
Perhaps they are dealing with situations that have nothing to do
with school,
Sounds strange,
To you maybe,
To me not,
Kids have a lot of luggage and school is the drop-off port for the
luggage because the parents have not checked the luggage,
Therefore, kids come to school with more than a backpack and lunch,
There is hope,
A listening ear and attention.

Service

Thank you,
God,
For all that you've done,
And continue to do for me,
And humanity,
Never do I wonder about your love,
You God,
Have always provided me with what I needed,
Your love,
Thank you,
God,
I will continue to serve you,
Not judging others,
Not placing labels on people,
I will serve you as my job on this planet.

Sickness

It's 4:00 a.m.,
Slept on sofa,
I manage to get into the bed,
10:46 a.m.,
The sound of a text message wakes me,
I'm not feeling all that great,
Sinuses,
A Cold,
Nerves,
Whatever it is, God, heal me,
I eat breakfast,
The phone rings,
Grandma is on the phone,
Grandpa is going back to the hospital,
He was up talking then he leaned over and turned blue,
We are in the ambulance now,
Okay,
I'm so afraid I think to myself,
God, help us,
I'm on my way I say,
Several hours pass,
I'm still at home,
Finding it hard to move but I must,
Grandma calls again,
How are you,
Grandpa has oxygen mask; Doc think it's a clot; will be admitted to
ICU; he's taking medication for clots now,
The rain is coming down,
Andy loves the rain,
I must go now to the ER,
God, watch over all your children.

Grandpa's Place

Upstairs,
At Grandma and Andy's,
Spending more time here since Andy's been admitted to hospital,
Talking and watching TV,
Tonight the Judds were on *Larry King*,
Lisa Presley on *Oprah* and a preview of Barbara Streisand on
Larry King,
Grandmother really enjoys the Judds,
I simply like them the mother-daughter dynamic; it's amazing,
Midnight arrives,
We prepare for bed,
I get the bed ready in the guest room,
Grandma makes her bed with freshly washed linens,
You can sleep with me,
The thought truly sweet

A Familiar Routine

My nerves have been rattled,
Yet I've not went to gym,
My nerves have almost gotten the best of me,
Yet I've give into my weakness,
Food,
A few weeks ago it started with a slice of pizza there,
Another slice of cheese pizza,
Then the next day tacos with cheese,
This is not good for my body, I know; too much dairy irritates my
allergies,
Here I am in the same place,
I must do better by living each day better,
I must not give in when things get rough,
Food is meant for nourishment and not abuse,
Even when I eat the not so good things I don't feel better,
I must go to the basics writing for healing and guidance.

New Diagnosis

It has been one month and ten days,
Since Grandpa left home,
Arthritis turned into gout,
Gout,
Next infection in bloodstream,
Much pain to follow,
Surgery occurs to flush out infection,
Extended stay at the hospital,
Things start to quiet down,
Andy goes to nursing home to learn how to walk,
Grandma visits daily,
During a visit,
Andy leans over and turns blue,
Off to the hospital,
We discover that there are clots in Grandpa's chest,
A few days in ICU Grandpa spends,
Then an extended stay at hospital,
Next stop back to nursing home,
The nursing home,
No different from where our animals are raised,

The treatment at times incomprehensible,
Some staff, nice,
Others, not so nice,
Grandpa wants out,
We want out for Grandpa,
Today is Tuesday,
Grandpa was to come home Wednesday,
He's not feeling well,
When I pick up Grandma, I learned docs want to keep him,
Grandma is drained,
I see her discomfort,
God, please heal all that are suffering,
Bring peace and rest to all,
Dear God, please allow all to rest.

MJ 23

Out for brunch,
Wishbone,
Down the street from Harpo Studios,
With the family,
Myself, aunt, uncle, my honey, and nephew,
Situated by the windows,
Enjoying conversation,
The meal is complete,
Restroom time,
I decline at first,
Then change my mind,
Upon walking by the bar,
Oh my,
Girl, what,
Michael Jordan is at the bar,
Back to the table we arrive,
Everyone is beaming from the news,
My honey stands up and heads to the bar,
I send nephew to the restroom and tell him to walk slow,
My honey has no fear,
My honey has the presence that wakes any room,
My honey goes to MJ and introduces himself and explains his
interest in all he's done,
He says to MJ I'd like you to meet someone,
Li'l David Mullons,
Li'l Dave extends a hand,
And MJ says nice to meet you.

Snowed In

Two days since the blizzard,
20 inches,
Lake Shore Drive closed down,
Hundreds of cars stuck in the snow,
Power outages,
Dangerous winds,
Sleep didn't find me until 4:00 a.m.,
The sounds from the blizzard kept me up,
Grandmother is sound asleep,
The morning comes,
The winds are sleep,
The street resemble ski slopes,
Cars slide in the streets,
Residents of the community pose on Lake Shore Drive,
Snowflakes fall,
The city is quiet,
With so much going on outside I stay in,
Completing homework,
Nightfall,
Sleep is much better,
A new day arrives,
Grandma and I cruise through the city,
Snow is everywhere,
Pedestrians are falling yet getting up quickly,
No more snow has fallen.

Westside

30 days have passed,
Since starting my new job as a program coordinator,
Working with computers,
Working in a field I've always enjoyed,
Each day,
12:00 p.m. to 4:15 p.m.,
Doesn't feel like work,
Each day I travel to the west side of Chicago,
The west side of Chicago where I was raised,
The west side of Chicago where my grandparents integrated a
predominately Jewish community and had police escorts when
they moved in,
Grandma explains a Realtor knew a couple that wanted to move
and Granddad jumped on the opportunity,
The west side of Chicago where my parents lived one block away
from another,
Many memories about the west side, some sad, some not so sad.

Embrace

An embrace,
Between two lovers,
Arms wrapped around one another,
Eyes locked together,
The energy enclosed of two lovers,
Faces side by side,
The beard tickles your lover during every embrace,
The sensation of the embrace,
The sensation of skin on skin,
Sealed between two lovers,
Never wanting this embrace to end.

Come Inside

Still you lie,
As I climb,
Searching for your sweetness,
Your hands reach for me,
Discovering every curve,
Discovering every opening of my body,
I become lost in you,
As you enter me,
Over and over.

Sorry

On this day, I'm up early,
Sleep did not find me yesterday evening,
So anxious to have you back,
I missed you so much,
I wanted you,
Wanted to show you how much I missed you,
You finished dinner,
Watched a little TV,
Then prepared for bed,
The water steamed in the bathroom,
All cleansed we've become,
We lie in bed,
I massaging every part of your body,
Both of our bodies are relaxed,
I enjoy placing my hands on you,
You drift off to comfort,
We lie,
I watch you sleep peacefully,
My hearts joy,
I'm up early,
The sounds from an older building,
The radiator,
No, the heater?
The sound ... Cling! Cling!
The sound ringed through my body,
Sleep did not find me,
I watched you sleep and sleep found me through you,

The sound interrupts my sleep again,
You are out like a light,
I try to get your attention,
You are peacefully resting,
I grab my rob and sit in the living room,
You do not ask for me,
I return,
You wake,
Reaching for me,
I continue to sit up,
G,
Come here,
I refuse,
Look at me,
I don't,
You look so sexy,
I refuse to lie with you,
Not wanting you to leave for work,
Not wanting you to let me go from your grasp,
Not wanting you to make me feel good, then stop,
I explain how the noise kept me up,
I don't explain that I wanted you but realized you were exhausted
from your travels,
You get up,
I lay down my head on your pillow,
You come and kiss me then caress and massage me,
I'm sorry for not lying with you,
I'm sorry I must change.

Work Day

My eyes are heavy,
Body aches,
Loving working with computers,
Not loving supervising people,
Nothing personal,
Various challenges,
Far beyond anyone's control,
Institutional problems,
What I can do to make the best of this situation,
Be inspiring,
Give my best each day,
These kids are special,
These kids deserve so much more,
The end of the workday approaches,
Lots going on,
I spend the day creating a form and visiting a 6th-grade class,
Troubleshooting tasks I enjoy,
During the end of the day, huddle, it's info distribution time,
My eyes are itchy,
I'm getting through the materials while voices are going,
Phones are ringing,
Lack of courtesy from some,
I announce how I need attention in order to share information,
Silence comes,
A few facilitators check on me after the huddle,

I'm okay; it's just irritating while voices are heard while speaking,
I avoid Lake Shore Drive,
Find western,
Stop by Mr. Submarine for turkey sandwich,
Chipotle for Grandma,
Visit with Grandpa,
I listen while venturing to North Carolina and Grandpa's days as
a worker,
Assembling pipes,
Learning of his challenges when working with people,
Gloria, you have to be patient with people,
Yes, Grandpa,
Color doesn't matter,
People are people,
I hear you,
Grandma says Grandpa has to have prostate surgery although it's
an outpatient procedure,
Dear God, be with us,
Sleep finds all humans tonight and keeps us safe along with all
God's creatures.

Love Lingers

My eyes open,
The window blinds are closed,
You are sound asleep,
The alarm clock sounds,
I kiss your shoulder,
Then your nose,
You look at me,
I look at you,
Our eyes setting the next scene,
My hands travel underneath the covers,
Finding your body,
Finding your pleasure spots,
Exploring you like a tourist in an unfamiliar city,
Going and going,
Smiling and moaning,
Going through the day high on you,
High on us,
Each moment I get to close my eyes I take it,
Immediately get comfortable after arriving home,
Napping finds me, I'm still high,
My eyes are heavy,
I love loving you.

Long Day

The day is still going,
The morning went by fast,
I washed my hair,
Now I feel so fresh,
The clock is rolling,
Time for work,
Grandparents are okay,
I pack a PB&J sandwich,
Peel a grapefruit,
Grab some water,
Head to the door,
No LSD today,
Construction work on 290,
Western Ave. is my alternate route,
The sun is shining,
It's truly a beautiful day,
Potholes are everywhere,
Work is not just work,
This job is my career,
I love technology and helping people,
End of the day, huddle,
Concerns about security,
Students, you name it, and it's voiced,

290 is my alternate route home,
A little congestion,
Arrive at parking lot,
Found a spot on level 2 and not 6,
I choose the stairs down to lobby,
Class starts,
Oh, I would like to take this bra off,
Sometimes I just want to rip it off,
At first I thought maybe a man invented the bra, but I changed
that thought,
It was Mary Phelps Jacobs, a New York socialite, who invented the
bra in 1913,
Oh, my bra was ready to come off,
As soon as I get home, I released my bra and breathed a deep sigh
of relief.

Food

Another struggle,
Deep-fried chicken wings with mild sauce,
In a moment I decide to eat this,
Knowing it is not right,
The first bite always tasty,
The second,
Then third,
Before I know it, the fourth piece gone,
Sitting in my stomach,
Taking three days to clear my system,
By the end of the day I've walked it off,
Feeling nauseous afterward,
Why do I do this,
I know I have a habit,
When I pray I ask to release the spirit of this animal to reside
with God,
Also I thank the life of this animal,
I eat out of habit,
At times I don't get this urge when I'm with my honey or doing
something I enjoy,
I've gotten my daily meat, fish, turkey intake to once, at the
maximum two, a day,
I feel better when I eat other things,
Each day is a struggle but I am doing the best I can,
I want to eat something because it's a meal or snack time and not
out of guilt,
Eating out of frustration,
Eating out of stress,
Eating out of anything that is not a meal or snack is detrimental
to my health.

Better Days

Times are getting better,
Grandpa is learning how to walk,
Grandma's cough has disappeared,
She's somewhat better,
Grandpa has a catheter,
No nurse helps Grandma,
Grandma and Grandpa don't want a nurse,
I see the wear on Grandma,
I run errands and help as much as I can,
Things are getting better,
People call to check on Grandma and Grandpa,
No visitors yet,
Only visitors are the nurse who checks on catheter and the
physical therapist,
And me,
Grandpa is getting stronger,
Caring for a loved one is a loving act.

Stronghold

Listening to,
Like the way you love me,
By Michael Jackson—2010,
Thinking about you,
And yesterday morning,
As we lie,
Sleeping,
Waking,
Chatting,
Cuddling,
Touching,
Exploring one another,
Legs wrapped closely around one another,
The strength of your touch excites me,
I'm weak,
Wanting you to never let go,
Keeping me safe,
The strength of your touch will always be with me.

I'm not the first

Could it be true,
That is what they say about love,
Doing things,
Things you probably never thought you'd be doing,
Things you probably never thought you'd never do,
Because of society's standards,
Don't live with a man before you're marriage,
Don't clean his house,
Don't cook,
Don't iron his clothes,
Keep your money; spend his,
The list is endless,
So what happens when you fall in love and you do all the above
and a little more,
Take time off from work to care for your lover,
Assume the role of caretaker out of love,
Anticipate your needs before you do,
Love you despite the lows and the low lows,
Not make an issue out of spending money as long as you have what
you need,
Provide a loving energy that ignites a flame,
Make you part of the family,
Blend a love together until time ticks out.

I Want You Settled

Out to dinner,
Red lobster,
Booth for two,
Grandma and I,
Dinner is delicious,
Service is excellent,
Conversation always enlightening,
Missy,
I just want you to settle,
As long as you are happy, Grandma says,
I understand,
It's been a few years,
Isn't it time for you to slow down on visiting so much,
I pause and think honestly,
Perhaps I should,
I've thought about it but don't do it,
Love has me doing all kinds of things,
Can't blame this on love,
Gloria is doing what she wants,
30 is my number,
Not sure why,
God, help me,
I'm settled where I am.

A Good Weekend

Weekdays,
Thursday being my favorite,
The thought of weekend approaching,
Relaxation with my honey,
This past weekend lovely,
Saturday I taught a class,
Building the business,
Absolutely fulfilling,
Saturday afternoon we get together,
Brunch,
Then a movie,
Ever notice the movie crowd on Saturday before 4:00 p.m. is
mellow and family-friendly,
The movie *Limitless* is a good pick,
Reviewers were not so favorable; however, the idea of taking a pill
to reach full intellectual capacity is interesting,
A visit to an aunt who loves the coat,
We hug and a tight embrace is captured,
Head to the market,
Vegetables, fruits, rice, milk, English muffins, and beets,
Pick up sandwiches from potbelly,

Server calls me; honey, you correct him and identify me as your wife,
I stand smiling at you,
Arrive at your place,
Shower,
Relax,
TV surf,
Morning arrives,
I make breakfast,
We feast on one another,
Nap periodically,
Head out to dinner,
Smile the entire meal,
Reflect upon the good weekend.

We Can

Marvin Gaye,
What's going on,
Much of the same,
Coupled with some change,
Schools across the US are screaming for help,
Kids are being pushed through the educational system with no tools,
Kids are frustrated,
What's going on,
War,
Air strikes against Libya,
The American educational system is at war with parents, teachers, and students,
Just the other day I got word of a student phoning a parent because something a security guard did to the student,
The parent came to the school with 10 other people and jumped the security guard,
What's going on, Marvin,
Much of the same,
What happened to the days when parents and teachers were on the same side,
What happened to the days when parents raised their children and taught the basics about respect and rules?
We got to wake up,
During slavery Africans were killed while learning to read,
Fast-forward today students sit in class reading behind grade levels,
What's going on,
We are at a pause and in need of serious intervention,
Marvin!
What's going on?

Will You Help Me

I step in a room to gather my notes,
A student is in the corner at a desk,
Eye contact is made,
I've seen this student before,
Upstairs in the hallway, awaiting dismissal,
I say, why are you in the hall,
ALO is finished,
I wanted to sit out here,
Okay, I say; however, you do understand this program is to help
you and we are here because we want you all to succeed,
Fast-forward back to the room,
After eye contact is made, the student says, will you help me,
Help you what,
A thesis,
Okay, I say,
What's your thesis,
I don't know what a thesis is,
I look down at student and give a generic definition,
The student goes on to explain assignment and reveals the thesis
that the teacher assigned although she can write another one as
long as she comes up with the topic,

We talk,
Her ideas flow freely,
A new thesis is created,
I'm a little surprised she asked for help,
She reminds me of myself,
The staff like her,
She helps with certain teachers,
I was the same way,
The highlight of my day,
Listening and talking to a student,
Later in the day the student saw me,
My teacher liked my paper,
I have another thesis for homework; it's a persuasive essay,
Great,
So you know you have to convince the reader about why MJ is the king of pop.

New Normal

The rain or perhaps sleet,
Coming down,
The coming to an end,
A day with great news,
No more catheter,
No more long hair,
Grandpa gets a haircut,
Such joy we have,
Things are getting back to normal,
A new normal,
We are so happy,
Grandma can relax a little better,
A perfect ending to a Thursday,
The rain or sleet.

Just Wait

At times, it seems like there's no help,
I think about whom I can call,
But if I just wait and listen,
I will have the help I need,

Hook:
I just wait,
When no one is around,
I just wait and ask for my purpose,
When no one can spell it out the way you do,
I just wait,
Know you see me through,
I wait,
Just wait,
For you.

It's not hard to do,
Just sit and ask or just listen,
Listen to the stillness of the moment,
If you believe of a divine power,
Greater than your boss,
Minister,
Or,
Clergy,
Just wait,
It will be revealed,
Once ask,
For what your purpose is in life,
Just wait,
Just wait and it will be revealed.

No Matter

You are my dream come true,
Many nights I prayed for you,
Often cannot believe you are real,
You are my dream come true and you're the real deal,

Hook—
No matter what people say we are a we,
No matter how people look at us, I'll always be your moon and you
my dream come true,
No mater what, no matter what,
You are my dream come true

Thought of You

Just the thought of you,
The thought of lovemaking,
Makes me want you more and more,
I feel you inside me,
Feel so in sync us,
Rain pouring outside,
Is this a dream,
You and me,
My body wakes,
I'm in bed alone,
Rain is beating on the window pane,
The feeling is real so real,
Making love,
Having leftovers . . .

Lorraine's Missy

An evening at home,
The day has come to an exhausting end,
Rent is ready,
I forget to put gown in cleaners for graduation,
Grandma is preparing chili,
The aroma is simply delightful,
How was your day,
I began To explain,
Details about the day,
Taste the chili,
I do,
Not too spicy,
Not bland,
Just right as usual,
My honey loves Grandmother's chili,
My honey loves Grandmother,
Grandmother is my teacher,
At times I've had to swallow things I'd rather not,
But Grandmother is always right,
Love has no rules,
The heart falls in love, and bam,
Nature takes its course,

I love being in love,
I'm in love with a man who is older than I,
Although we have much in common,
We both are passionate about public service,
We both are passionate about God, the universe music, history,
and so much more, I'm in love with a man who I know was sent
from God and made specifically for me on this particular stage of
my journey,
I'm in love with a man I asked God to send me,
A man who believes in God, loves himself and humankind,
I've asked God to reveal to me what to do,
Stay with him the voice came so clearly one night,
We have weathered some storms, my honey and I,
Being in love is a journey for two while people watch and admire
your relationship.

God, Please Help Me

At times my thoughts run my brain rapid,
Endless thoughts of nothing positive,
God, please help me to stay in the moment and not hurt others,
I'd rather not cause pain,
God, please help me respond and not react to my ego,
Each month my period shakes up my emotions and I question my
current relationship although I shouldn't,
I question what we are doing and where we're going,
Each month,
The same thought resurfaces,
God, is this a sign from you? Or could I be missing the lesson,
God, I ask that you please reveal my purpose with this man,
Is it time to change seasons,
Was I only to help him get through a difficult point in his life,
Is it time for me to let go,
God, please help me,
Reveal my purpose,
God, please don't let my emotions run me into a place that I will
lose sight of what I'm supposed to do.

Time to cruise

Up by 10:00 a.m.,
Temperature already 85 degrees,
Flip the AC on,
Fix my hair,
Eat strawberries and drink water for breakfast,
Press a jacket,
Get dressed,
Drop Sunday paper to Grandma,
Leave with Grandma's hat,
Feeling pretty,
Head south,
Some traffic going southbound,
Arrive at destination,
Chit chat,
The heat is on for real,
We leave and head to navy pier,
I'm a little irritable but I apologize,
Entering lot and instead of words my honey makes a funny sound
that I cannot explain,
Later he explains, a car coming out of a park,
I apologize for making the sound,
We board the boat,
I'm feeling so-so,
We find a table and introductions are made,
This is my friend,
What?
Don't take this personal, Gloria,
I'm his friend,

All kinds of thoughts flash through my mind like a serious headache,
Yes, we are friends, that's a given,
We also are intimate and so much more,
In public in certain social gatherings, I'm your friend,
In private, I'm your baby,
Your sweet thang,
Your moon,
Yet in public you feel the need to label what we are,
I'm tired of this,
The afternoon intensifies,
Fundraisers are walking around and you are sucking on a drink
and didn't bother to order me water,
At any rate they ask you about purchasing a raffle ticket and you
salivate with excitement or could it be the attention,
They see your money and you just smile and let a woman put a
magnet on your shirt,
I turn away thinking she can have your ass,
Have some respect,
Decline the assistance out of respect for me,
Don't take this personal, Gloria,
The entire evening I watch your eyes as they watch women walk
across the room and I watch the men and wonder what things
would be like if we were not together.

Sweet Love

An end to the evening,
Brings about sweetness,
The beauty of lovemaking,
Hands roaming,
Roaming through your world,
Exploring all the fantasies you have,
Climbing,
Climaxing,
Arching,
Grasping your hands,
Watching you smile in pleasure,
Basking in sweet love,
Sweet love exchanged between us,
Us reaching new sweet love between us

Midnight munchies,

Midnight has arrived,
Clothes for work ironed,
Dishes washed,
Floor swept,
I resist the urge to munch on Double Stuff Oreos,
I've eaten plenty . . . a mini turkey sandwich, oatmeal pie, chicken,
and tips,
To top the evening off a drumstick,
I've showered,
Now I will read and rest,
Good night.

Happy the Way Things Are

I take it back,
Not really,
Happy the way things are,
Wanting more,
Is it wrong,
Living under the same roof,
Waking and sleeping together,
Sharing precious moments,
Happy the way things are but reality has set in,
Who's reality is it wanting to be married,
Who's to say I won't come up with something else I want,
It's easy to want and crave,
Happy the way things are,
Loving you,
Waking up to you,
Sharing evenings with you,
Being your best friend,
Loving you for who you are in this moment,
Happy the way things are but I've dreamed of my wedding day if
that's what God has in store.

Hair Time

A long work week ends,
Mother Nature has arrived,
A salon visit contemplated,
K-mart is visited,
Glasses,
Bread,
Household cleaning products,
Cookies for Grandpa,
Chips and graham crackers for me,
It's light when I enter the store,
Dark when I leave the store,
My legs are aching from yesterday's food drive at work,
Finally home I arrive,
The taco shells from store ruins my chili but I continue eating,
The sofa calls my name,
Sleep finds me while Grandma watches *General Hospital*,
It's now midnight; I've slept for 30 or 60 minutes,
Ready to wash my hair,
Release all my clothes,
Comb through my hair and smile,
Run hot water all over my body, letting my fingers run through
my hair,

After two washes, feeling good and calm,
Add some conditioner,
Finger hair as I comb,
Rinse out and shower,
Feeling so good,
Dry hair,
Decide on a different style,
Part hair into four sections,
Apply some cream and 2 strain twist, here we come,
Not sure what the outcome will be, but I am excited about trying
something different,
My honey phones from LA while I'm twisting,
He's so sexy,
Wishing I took him up on the trip,
I miss him already but happy he is doing what he enjoys,
I love him very dearly.

Loving My Man

Reflecting on our day together a true gift,
Running errands together,
Cleaners,
Car shopping,
Grocery shopping,
Eating breakfast and ordering different menu items,
Green tea,
Eggs, pancakes, and turkey links,
I've been dealing with allergies the past few days, but as always,
you are my special love in this world,
Loving you brings me so much joy,
At times I want to cry,
You have allowed me the opportunity to love you unconditionally,
My heart, soul, and spirit smiles because of you,
I am so content with our life,
No matter what I share about others thoughts,
I am so content with our life and how we are living it,
At times I make comments about children and marriage only to
see the look in your eyes,
Heck, who wouldn't want to start a life with you,
I am so content in this moment that we have together.

Date Night

The day ends with rain,
I love the sound and smell of rain,
My body relaxes,
Date night,
Really sweet with my honey,
Walking arm in arm,
Smiling at one another,
Sharing the events of the day,
O love sitting across from my hone, drinking a shot of Johnny
Walker with a Samuel Adams,
Me eating turkey gobblers and smiling while listening to my honey,
The time for *Moneyball* arrives,
A true story based on the baseball and how projections come to be,
My honey is glowing,
I want to escape away and make love,
My honey ignites passion in me,
During a scene in the movie a little girl sings while playing a guitar,
I wanted a little girl, my honey says,
I'm lost for words,
I'm also on my period and feeling very nurturing,
The day ends on a high note.

Non stop

My body aches,
What a whirlwind of a day,
8:00 a.m. at school,
10:00 a.m. at corporate office,
1:00 p.m. at center,
2:00 p.m. back at school for afternoon programming,
The entire program spent with a group of little people,
1st task homework,
It's challenging engaging students but there I was,
Homework is checked,
Next task,
Dominoes,
Learning to identify numbers,
Create addition problems,
Task complete,
Kids are full of energy,
Kids are ready to relax and let loose,
I slowly simmer down,
Next task, the computer lab,
Kids are naturally excited and rowdy,
Going to all kinds of sites not prohibited,
Rewind during classroom time the janitor came upstairs and
complained about the noise and explained that after-school is a
privilege,
I just sat and listened,
The students responded to some of his questions sparingly,

At this point my body aches,
I've had several pieces of Starburst candy,
The day is almost over,
I sit in my car with my shoes off, eating a banana from Ms. Frazier
or the lady with the locks,
I'm so blessed that God has placed me on this journey,
Use me, God, for my purpose,
Cover me in your light,
Home I finally make it,
Dinner,
Leftover greens, sweet potatoes, fish, and sliced tomatoes,
God, thank you for my grandma as we sit and talk about the day's
events,
I love being home,
I love home,
Thank you, God.

Out for the Holidays

This past Saturday,
We hit the town,
My side,
North side,
A Christmas at Nookies,
8:00 p.m.,
Parking is limited,
We circle for close to 30 minutes,
Finally a spot opens on Bryn Mawr,
A brisk walk less than a Chicago block,
Coats are checked,
Intros and hellos flow throughout the restaurant,
Some familiar faces,
Some new faces,
A splendid evening with a live band,
Cozy seating in a booth style setting,
Caramelized carrots, baked brussels sprouts, salad, smothered
nuggets and other meat,
We sit,
People watch,
Make small talk with other folk,
We stand and listen to the band,
Side by side,
Then my honey moves behind me,
Begins whispering in my ear and holding my hand,
Talking sweet in my ear,
I'm blushin'.

We crawl into bed,
Our bodies find our connecting spot,
My backside nestled in your lap,
Your chin I feel in the nape of my neck,
Our temperature rise,
We remove our layers,
We find ourselves entangled,
Arms,
Legs,
Lips,
Wrapped up together in a sweet tune,
Assuming the position of lovemaking,
Cuddling,
Sleep arrives,
Morning comes,
Our bodies yearn for seconds,
We indulge, not wanting to stop,
Discovering new paths,
Moaning in, yes, baby.

Lunch time

A work day has ended,
A busy one,
Data entry,
Checking e-mails,
Helping coworkers,
Printing labels,
Greeting families with Christmas gifts,
My nose is running like a faucet,
When will I learn my lesson,
Lunchtime arrives,
Subway it is,
Veggie patty,
I get lunch for Ms. T,
A hardworking lady,
Warms my heart to treat others,
The day ends,
Feel 75 percent better leaving center,
Run a few errands,
Give a homeless person $15,
Head home,
Get ready for the evening.

Insurance Companies

Insurance Companies,
All about profits,
Nauseous to my stomach,
Insurance companies take advantage of seniors,
Give them drugs,
Pressure them to make decisions.

February

Lou Malnati's
The day has finally come to a halt,
I open the door to my grandparents place,
Delivery in hand,
Damn,
The door slams,
Lights are out,
Only the sound of the radio can be heard,
Grandma is napping, I think
Grandpa is in bed,
Did you eat? I ask Grandma,
No,
I have some pizza and salad,
I get plates,
And explained about my craving for this salad,
The dressing is delicious,
We eat,
Both enjoying the company and meal,
We sit this way for hours,
The beauty in listening,
My grandma is one of a kind,
I feel so blessed to be in her midst,
Her existence is golden,
Life is grand when you're a granddaughter,
Learning firsthand.

I Wonder

Things are good,
But I wonder sometimes,
Wonder about the future,
The unknown,
All we have is the moment that exists,
I wonder how long will we dance this step,
I love you dearly,
I've prayed to God and the universe for you,
Now I have you and I wonder,
I wonder what I'd be doing if we were not together,
I wonder if I would ever find a love like yours,
Sometimes wondering is dangerous,
I'm very blessed as to what I have in my life,
Sometimes I wonder perhaps when things get tough or when life
seems too predictable; I wonder but then I get a jolt,
A reality check to bring me back into the real world,
Sometimes I wonder,
Thank goodness for a pen and paper because once I wonder and
write, gone are the thoughts about the what-ifs and maybes.

Crave My Lover

On a not so cold night,
I crave being in the arms of my lover,
The kitchen is calling,
My lover is 30 minutes away,
I want him so,
To feel his arms around my hips,
His head in my chest,
Our bodies in a groove.
On a not so cold night I crave my lover.

Day 3 on the New Job

Saucedo elementary school,
Huge building,
Not far from the county jail California Street,
Checking a parenting class,
All staff on deck,
Mommies are present,
Paint dishes are being used,
Paper flowers are being assembled,
Before arriving to room a little birdie gives me the 411,
I quit the company after 6 months,
Interesting, I thought, or perhaps not,
I've heard the county was like revolving doors,
Now I hear the same thing in the nonprofit sector,
What's going on?
I believe everything happens for a reason,
It was meant for me to meet this little birdie who shared her experiences with me,
An older woman,
Who has seen many things,
The fact remains there are more participants in Saucedo than attendance at the center,
The world is changing,
Blacks who lived in Cabrini-Green are spread out,
Hispanics are increasing and becoming the leading culture in terms of population,
We must learn how to work with one another,
This reminds me of the digital divide and in some cultures not using the Internet because of language barriers; we have got to move past this stage and educate ourselves about other cultures.

Graduate School Graduation

Day after master's graduation,
I'm tired,
Woke up tired,
Fixed breakfast,
Gathered belongings,
Head to garage,
Grandma is waiting,
41 South is crowded; this is normal,
I feel stressed,
Have to be in line by 9:40 a.m.,
Off we go on Halsted to North Avenue, then Ashland,
Find a spot in the street and my honey feeds the meter after I
decide not to enter lot at his recommendation, knowing card
access is the only entry except for graduation day,
A nice ceremony,
The sun is shining,
Speakers are nice overall,
Grandma is beaming,
Honey feeds the parking meter,
After the ceremony is over I see my brother,
A true surprise,
Have lunch at Uncle Julio's,
Pick up lunch for grandpa at Chipotle
Take a nap,
Watch news,
Head to target with honey,
Pick up some summer clothes for niece and nephew,
Feeling dizzy,
Eat leftover Chinese,
I should rest,
Decide to have a snack,
Now it's time for bed

Tinley Park Training

Off to training in Tinley Park,
Up at 5:00 a.m.,
On CTA 145 by 6:15 p.m.,
The lake is beautiful,
My eyelids blink occasionally,
Arrive at the financial district,
Make my descent up the stairs I slip but catch my fall and remain
on my feet,
A lady asks if I'm okay,
Very thoughtful of her,
The ride is nice and quick,
Once I arrive in Tinley Park, I spark up a conversation about
getting to 7550 W. 183rd Street, I'm getting a little lost but have a
wonderful walk around the metro station,
I make it finally,
First day of training is exciting but gets dry after lunch,
We let out early and I'm ecstatic.

Summer Camp

Blessed to have another day,
Up early,
Press the snooze button for a bit,
Not wanting to leave the warmth and comfort of my home,
Breakfast is fresh strawberries that my 77-year-old grandma has
rinsed and carved for me,
I am so fortunate to have my grandmother,
Life is truly good,
Summer camp is underway,
Each day I'm getting to know the kids better,
Arriving home is a treat,
My feet scream for the hardwood floors to soothe them,
My eyelids are heavy, waiting for closure,
The trees are gently blowing,
The cars are slowly driving on Lake Shore Drive,
Body aches from a long day,
My dentist wants to fill another cavity on the 21st,
Gave her a book and I thought she almost cried,
Helped a coworker set up an e-mail account on smartphone and
an account on Walgreens,
A beautiful day it has been,
Now it's time to relax and enjoy my favorite seat in the house on
the sofa.

Chantz

Dinner for 2,
Low-lit restaurant in Hyde Park,
Iced Thai tea for me and a beer for you,
Asparagus roll appetizers,
Stimulating conversation,
Eye contact,
Smiling,
Rubbing of the arms,
Listening with our eyes,
Delicious shrimp curry,
One dessert for 2,
Red velvet cake,
You and I,
Lounged all day,
Watched the History Channel,
Discovered slaves were given cocaine to work productively,
according to historians,
Definitely didn't know about that before today,
Cocaine was introduced back in the 1800s or 1900s,
Reintroduced with crack in the black community,
Hitler high, another piece about drug use,
Hitler's doctor traveled with him 24-7.

Damn

Today turned out to be one of those days,
Slept in late,
Not too excited about the workplace picnic,
It's mandatory, so I can't get out of it,
The clouds are looking stormy,
It's getting dark,
I'd love to stay in bed,
No way I'm driving in this stuff,
I relax on sofa,
Check on grandparents,
Their AC had cardboard in it from the winter so when the house
didn't cool—naturally this was upsetting,
We were concerned about a fire,
All work out,
Off to work picnic,
I get lost thanks to Garmin and end up at Ford City Mall and not
the lake,
Gotta make a stop at the Golden Arches bathroom time,
There are clowns,
Arts and crafts,
The lake,
Mosquitoes,
After I shared my story as to why I was late, half a dozens times I
begin to wonder,
I've become one of those people that have a job so the bills can be paid,
I'm blessed for this job but, dear God, please help me work in an
area that you have chosen for me,
I'm concerned about the structure and lack of leadership,
God, help me continue to I've my best and not have not so good
thoughts about my current job.

Love Yourself

In life mistakes are made,
The mistakes does not define who we are,
Let the mistake be just that,
Don't fester in the not so good,
Learn from the mistake,
Don't beat yourself up and abuse yourself,
Love yourself at all times,
All on earth are to be happy and not miserable,
Only when self is loved first can we love others,
Amy Winehouse,
27 years old,
Dead,
Fame and fortune is nothing,
One must have fame and fortune in the heart and soul for self,
Not in materialistic things or drugs,
Only a hug can make you feel like another day is bearable.

My Mouth

Looks like all those candy bars and other junk food finally caught up with me,
Years of not flossing,
Finally caught up with me, so it seems,
When I was a kid, I recall going to the dentist,
As I got older, things changed,
Dental visits became rare,
But I continued to enjoy what gave me comfort—candy, potato chips, cupcakes, and whatever else tasted good,
If I wasn't in pain, I didn't see a doc,
I watched my mom suffer from toothaches and I told myself as I grew that I would always take care of my health and see a doctor on a regular basis,
Now I'm a grown woman and I've had braces and 2 cavities and working on an extraction,
I will clean my mouth better and have cleaner thoughts and actions toward people.

Day before Extraction

The pain woke me up,
I tapped into my spirituality,
God is my health,
Will the pain away,
Phone the dental office and medicine is prescribed after suffering the bulk of the weekend,
My grandma is always by my side,
After picking up prescriptions, I eat breakfast that Grandma has prepared,
We sit on the sofa and watch TV,
She's concerned about me,
My grandma is always there for me no matter what,
It's always beautiful to have a helping hand without asking for it,
Thank you, God.

Tooth Gone

Up by 6:00 a.m.,
Out the door by 7:15 a.m.,
Grandma and I on the bus headed downtown,
Get checked in by receptionist,
Nurse calls me to the back for an x-ray,
I'm all prepped,
Local anesthesia applied all while talking about computers, Excel, and media clips,
I couldn't believe all this was going on while the doc pulled my tooth from my jawbone,
I felt no pain,
The doc was cool and calm and played nice music while also talking about how my service is all on point for helping seniors and kids learn about technology . . . smartphones, cameras, computers, and anything else that's digital,
Doctor even mentioned something about a multibillion dollar friend who helps his 90-year-old mother with computers,
I walked out the room feeling okay,
Grandma was surprised at how I looked and behaved, she even asked if I'd had the procedure done,
We left all smiles,
Got on the bus and I use my spit bag in hiding,
Arrived at home for the car and went to breakfast,
The pancakes, hash browns, and turkey sausage, truly delicious,
Next stop CVS,
Home sweet home by 1:00 p.m.,
God is amazing,
I'm so blessed.

How I'm Feeling

Eyes closed,
Bodies singing the sweetest melody,
Feels good when you kiss my lips,
Then my neck,
I'm lost in the rhythm of our bodies,

Hook—
You make me want to cry out loud,
I can feel your love erupting in me,
I want to thank God for this energy,
Feeling your hands makes me want to dance forever with you and
only you

Sade Concert

United Center,
Section 108,
John Legend opens,
Show starts at 7:30,
John warms the crowd nicely,
Sade comes out around 8:30,
Sade rocks it,
Her wardrobe and stage presence lures you in,
The band is jumping.
All kinds of thoughts are running through my mind,
Like clockwork,
The same thoughts every month around my period,
Is this relationship for me?
Where is it going?
Am I just the help?
All thoughts in my mind,
These thoughts driving me crazy at times; they scream at me,
Dear God, help me,
Is our time up?
This has been a wonderful experience loving you through sickness
and good health,
Dear God, help me please.

A Trip

Hopped on a plane,
Enjoying the takeoff and landing,
A few years since coming west,
A joyous occasion it is,
Stayed at the Trump in a suite,
Got a few surprises,
Rolled with the punches, not wanting to judge anyone,
In life change is required,
Not all can embrace it but it's necessary,
Having exposure can make a world of a difference,
If all one sees is the same-ole, same-ole, then it can be challenging
seeing a different outcome,
In life change is required in order to grow,
I want the best for all,
This trip has been full of ups and downs,
It's 11:00 p.m.,
In Circus, Circus,
Reading,
Don't feel like playing any more machines,
Just waiting and reading,
Same-ole, same-ole,
I'm sitting at a slot machine,
Folks to my left a couple,
Guy to my right smoking a cigarette,
The machines are jumping for the folks on the left,
I think about moving but I don't.

Am I Dreaming

We start Saturday morning,
Sharing fruit,
Channel surfing,
Curled up in bed,
Touching,
Smiling,
Kissing,
We start day expressing our love,
Chest to chest,
Legs extended,
Lips exploring hidden sweetness,
I feel as if this is a dream.
I ask you if this is a dream,
Being in your arms after lovemaking feels magical,
I'm smiling all over.

Chitchatting

Women,
Chitchatting,
All kinds of questions going through my head,
Should I reveal this,
What will they think,
I don't care what they think,
I love this man,
So years later perhaps I will have the ending to this saga; as for now it's still brewing,
Chitchatting about my man,
I feel good talking about how he makes me happy,
I feel good about the pleasant weekend we had making love, being together, and reflecting on God,
I feel good knowing that we are a we,
Do I think about the future, of course,
Do I think about walking down the aisle,
Do I think about carrying a child,
All these thoughts cross my mind,
But I can only live in the God-given moment that's provided to me,
I can't be concerned about changing my life for someone else,
I can't let someone else's thoughts be my life,
Am I being naive,
Am I being gullible,
Who cares, I don't,
I'm in love,
So what if he doesn't pop the question when you think he should,
When I'm ready to make a change God will reveal to me,
I wanted this man because I visualized him and I ask God for him,
I'm in the midst of my lesson,
So far I've learned not to judge a person based on my own perceptions.

Living

Living is a gift,
At times life is too much,
Wanting to help everyone can be a lot,
Aren't we on earth to help fellow woman and man?
Living is a gift that is to be treasured,
At times I stop and slow down to wash my hair, clip my toenails too, iron some clothes, paint my nails, wash some dishes, clean the refrigerator, and sweep the floor,
At times I make lists of the little projects around the house; put away summer clothes, bring out the fall clothes, throw away or donate all the clothes I'm not wearing.
At times I want to write each day, but I don't always feel the spark that ignites me to write so I let this pass and relax.
Living is a gift to be shared with the person or persons you care about.

A Coat and a Hat

The warm sun woke me up,
I resisted by placing my arms over my face,
I eventually get up,
Clean the bathroom,
Clean my body,
Dress,
Head downtown with Grandma,
#146 bus was rolling down Lake Shore,
I jogged to the bus and told Grandma not to worry,
The bus was moderately filled for a Sunday afternoon,
I didn't see the lake due to where Grandma and I sat,
I did notice all the activity in the park,
Dog walking,
Fishing,
Jogging,
Festivals,
A fun-filled Sunday in the park,
The ride to the Magnificent Mile took 10 or 15 minutes,
Off the bus,
People are everywhere,
The sun and wind are . . .
Into the store we go,
The colors are bright,
How may we help you

A Pattern

Time goes on no matter what,
The days,
The weeks,
The months,
And years pass by,
Love will have people do strange things,
Stay in relationships that are going,
Just going no place exactly,
Love teaches,
Love makes you feel all sorts of things about lovers,
Love and put yourself first always.

Sound of Rain

Lying on the sofa,
All windows are open,
The breeze enters my home,
My thoughts drift to you,
The rain is coming down,
Your body covers my body,
Your lips plant sweet kisses on my neck,
We kiss,
You find your comfort and settle,
Rocking nice and slow just how I like it,
My body smiles,
I lie on the sofa,
Remembering our sweet moments,
Wishing you were with me right now,
I crave you.

Milwaukee

The day started off as a gift like every previous day,
Short day at work,
Very productive,
Off at 2:00 p.m.,
Pick up my meds,
Head home,
Talk about my day with Grandma,
Play the Wii game with Nephew,
Gotta pack,
Time is speeding by,
Train leaves at 8:05 p.m.,
My first trip taking my niece and but not my nephew on a trip out
of Illinois,
They are tired yet anxious.

Time

For some time this has been on my mind,
Oftentimes I just ignore it,
The constant thought of where is this going,
Am I not living in the moment?
I can't seem to stop the thoughts that I have,
Surely I have known that the time would come,
I'm sure that I will always love you,
A true gentleman you are,
I thank God for this opportunity to love you and be loved by you,
Dear God, please help me to not want for materialistic things,
God, allow me to continue to want what you have planned for my
purpose on this planet,
I am all yours and dedicate my life to you,
I yearn for my purpose,
I realize that the greatest gift is to give love to self and others,
Dear God,
Continue to keep and heal me,
Dear God, for I love you more than my life and I ask you to take
charge of my life,
Dear God, I love you and thank you for making me,
Keep me.

Midnight

40 degrees,
It's November,
Snuggled closely,
Your face nestled next to mine,
Arms entangled,
We are volcanoes erupting at midnight,
Simmering at dawn,
Basking in the glow by noon,
Smiling,
Talking,
Loving the moments from yesterday's midnight.

Errands

A rainy Saturday morning,
Relaxing around the house,
Made a grocery list,
Ran some errands with Grandma and my niece,
The rain didn't stop,
In and out of stores,
Girl talk and shopping,
Grab lunch at home together,
Visit Grandpa,
Watch Cartoon Network,
A true gift this Saturday running errands.

Old Habits

The past few weeks,
Have not felt like writing much,
Instead I've reverted to old habits,
Munchies,
Flamin' hots,
Popcorn,
Candy,
Hot wings,
You name it and I've sampled,
A few years ago I discovered what helps when I'm a little
overwhelmed or stressed,
Writing about my day regardless of what happened ensuring that
I keep it raw or put a positive spin on things,
The past few weeks I haven't written how things have been going
in my life and I've paid a small price,
I've had a dairy overdose,
Had to take antibiotics,
Been down this road before,
God, please help me,
I don't want to cause illness within.
God, guide my life.

3:00 a.m.

Eyes open,
Hands headed below the surface,
The deep waves make way ashore,
It's 3:00 a.m.,
Why are we not together,
Thoughts of you awaken me,
It's 3:00 a.m. and I'm wondering why my body is calling for you,
Missing you,
Needing you.

January

It is a new year,
I must do things differently,
Check the attitude and negativity,
Be ready for the bigger plan God has in store for me,
Be a better servant to others,
Love all and not let *but* get in my way,
No excuses!
New thinking,
Expanded space for God and his plan for me,
I am governed by the laws of God,
Health, spirit, and wealth are my birth right as an heir of God.
I will seek the Holy Spirit for counsel about whom to talk to,
I will mediate more.
Am awesome day in church—lecture bondage.

Disagreement

A conversation about educational thoughts,
Think about this area,
Well, I suppose; however, I don't plan on being in the field much longer.
Conversation changes,
Tone changes,
I gaze out the window,
Apparently this does not sit well with you,
You express your concluding thoughts and exit the living room,
Look out the window, you say,
I sit,
All kinds of thoughts go through my head,
It's a new year,
So we have a misunderstanding due to different views,
We kiss,
Smile,
Talk a little more trash,
You take clothes out of washer,
We chat,
On my way down a resident, ask me if I'm going outside,
I say yes, pointing to another direction,
Letters are in his hand,
But you are going outside? That's okay.
I look at him,
Exit the elevator and meet the hawk.
20 degrees.

After school programs

A long day comes to an end,
My body aches,
Feet are throbbing,
Working with kids.
It takes a special soul to work with kids,
2 hours I spend with them,
Sounds short and simple,
At times it is, yet some days it's just rough,
Plain rough,
Anger spills out of the mouths,
Curse words fill the room,
A long day comes to an end,
Kids go home,
I reflect,
Listen to music and soak in a long hot bath.
Dear God, give me the strength.

Happy Birthday

Happy 78th b-day,
Today this beautiful day,
My sweet grandma turned 78,
A beautiful day,
Horseshoe casino,
The buffet was awesome,
Saw Liz and Charles Cotton,
Sold 8 books,
A wonderful day on Grandma's 78th b-day.

Programming

Another Monday,
Kids are rambunctious
Snacks handed out,
Eyes lurking through the windows,
What are we doing?
The lab is where we end up,
Go to the school site and do something educational,
Repeat same message over and over,
Program almost over,
Words exchanged between a 5th grader and an 8th grader,
I restrain the 8th-grade male,
The 5th-grade girl continues to tease the 8th grader.

Not NW but NLU

Wednesday, February 8, 2012
Dear Gloria,

After consultation with the African-American Studies: PhD (A13PH) program and after a thorough evaluation of your credentials by the graduate school, I regret to inform you that you have been denied admission for graduate study at Northwestern University.

Because your interest in the university is deeply appreciated, this decision is not easy to convey. Though your plans cannot be accommodated at Northwestern University, the faculty and administrators of the graduate school respect your intellectual ambition and wish you success in attaining your goal of advanced study.

Sincerely yours,
Dwight A. McBride, PhD
Dean of the Graduate School and Associate Provost for Graduate Education

Student Name: Gloria Danielle Mullons

Whitney

I'm driving to a dance recital,
Listening to the radio 102.7,
The announcement comes through the radio,
Whitney Houston dead at 48,
All previous thoughts disappear,
What happened? Are my initial thoughts,
Feb. 12,
The morning after the death of Whitney Houston,
As a little girl,
I loved Whitney Houston,
The first movie I saw on cable was *The Bodyguard*,
I loved the movie so much that I wrote the sequel,
I never turned it in to Hollywood,
There was only 1 TV in the house with cable,
My grandparents room at 4040 West Cullerton
Whitney inspired me,
I would sing all the time around the house,
My grandma Hattie would tell me, "Go in the bathroom and close
the bathroom door and sing, girl!,"
I would sing to the top of my lungs,
I simply loved Whitney Houston,
One day I sang for Grandma Lorraine at her house at 4107 W.
Cullerton Street,

My brother David, said "Grandma, Gloria, can sing,
Grandma Lorraine bought me 2 radios with the duo cassette
players and I would play music while recording my voice,
To this day Grandma still says, I thought you would sing,
I probably would have but I just didn't,
To this day I sing when I can and when I need to let off some steam,
God, music and writing will always be my therapy,
Whitney was a true role model for me,
I will never forgot babysitting my aunt Louise's poodle, Poochie,
in LA,
I watched a video of Whitney performing for the troops on a ship
and like the troops, I enjoyed the show,
Surely I shed a tear from the performance while watching responses
from the troops,
Regardless of what was going on in her life, I never stop loving
who she was as a person,
My heart was sad from what she was going through in life but I
always felt inspired by her as a person,
When she was married and *Ebony* profiled her wedding, I read the
article over and over while imaging I was a guest at the wedding,
Whitney a true gift,
Whitney your life exemplified grace and beauty,
Whitney I dreamed because of you,
Whitney I will always love you.

Help Me

Help me, dear Lord,
Slipping into old habits,
I am stronger than this,
Craving,
Eating snacks,
I will overcome these cravings,
I crave you, Lord,
Guide me,
I believe I will get better,
Place before me what you see for me,
God, you are all I need,
I do believe that, God, you are the perfect path for my life.

Green Beans

Last night,
Stopped by the store,
Picked up some fresh green beans,
Got home,
Kicked my shoes off,
Pulled out Grandmother's cookbook,
Googled instructions on cooking string beans first,
Needing Grandmother's cookbook, wanting to get things done a certain way,
I love using Grandmother's cookbook
 I really feel like a grown woman,
I even stood over the table and read,
Lord, you have instilled Grandmother's ways in me. . .
I stand over the sink,
Rinse the green beans,
And snap the ends,
Snap,
Snap,
Snap,
Rinse, rinse,
All while the water is boiling,
I enjoy the kitchen creating especially after a long day,
The water soon began to boil,
I placed the beans in the pot and sprinkled some onion and garlic pepper,
This is relaxing,
I check on the green beans,
A taste here and there,
Too firm,
Let's cook a little longer,
Another taste they're ready!
Today I made green beans for my honey.

Patience

There isn't much I can do,
I want to help,
What can I do,
Be patient,
Realize this is something you need to work through,
I care for you so much,
I realize my idea of helping is not helping you,
I wait and am patient,
Been down this road before,
Love will keep us but space and time is what you need right now.

Non stop

Up by 6:24 a.m.,
Watch my honey sleep,
Get cleaned up and make breakfast,
Off to work,
Then the airport,
Swing by the center,
Head to school for afternoon programming,
Deal with the kids who are being sent out of class,
Pick Grandma up from the bus stop on Polk and Western,
Head to Old Country Buffet with Grandma, David, and the kids,
Make it home; I'm exhausted,
A wonderful day.

Car Hit

A beautiful windy day is over,
A quick errand before going home,
Parked the car in a space,
Fumble with my phone,
See a light from the rearview mirror,
Return to my phone,
The light fades,
I hear a loud sound and feel the impact of it,
My left panel is hit!
I get out of my car,
The driver pulls into a space,
I'm looking at him as he hesitates getting out of the car,
I motion where the damage is,
He looks and says, was there any other damage,
I said to myself, heck no,
He pulls out his phone and starts dialing,
I'm in shock,
I remain cool,
We exchange info,
The guy chases his info through the light as it has been blown out
of his hand,
I talk to the claims rep who indicate I will hear something in 2 days,
I manage to enter the store and retrieve the items needed for the
morning parents program,
I head home,
Thank you, Lord,
For keeping me cool,
It's just a car and no one was hurt.

Hair cut

Ready to do it,
Cut it all off,
Ready to change it for real,
I've always had long hair,
Turning 30 this year,
Thought about locks,
Or just cutting it really short and tapering in the back,
Want to rub the back of my head,
Wash my hair,
Feel the water run through my scalp,
Want my hair to air dry,
Ready for a change.

Missing each other

Days go by,
I miss you in the sweetest way,
You are working,
I am working,
When we are apart, I reflect,
I reflect on the beauty of what we have,
Your smile lightens my chaotic day,
Missing you strengthens me,
Strengthens our relationship,

Costa Rica

Day 1—slept most of the flight,
So tired after staying up the previous evening,
We landed in Liberia,
Lots of transportation companies wanting to take us to our destination,
We manage to get with Alamo Company and we get to our rental,
What started off a simple journey to our lodging turned into an adventure,
Roads with few signs,
Bumpy roads,
Unpaved roads,
Now we're driving for 2 hours,
We stopped to get water and Cokes,
The drive is longer than expected,
Just when we think that we've arrived,
A wrong turn leads us to a beach,
A white sandy beach,
A white sandy beach that traps us in the sand,
The locals help us by placing wood underneath the wheels,
We managed to get out,

Day 2 of Costa Rica,
Slept wonderfully,
Went to be bed with the sounds of nature,
Woke up,
Feeling relaxed,
Skin looks clearer,
Sat in bed and chitchatted,
Got cleaned up,
Loaded up and headed down the hill,
Breakfast at the Luna Azul,
Fresh orange juice,
Fruit,

Bread and marmalade . . . mango, papaya, lime, banana, eggs, and
rice with green tea,
Headed into town,
I could see my honey relaxing, with no TV or gadgets,
Just us,
Feeding on one another,
Wish you were here,
I woke up from a dream and you were kissing me,

Day 3 in Costa Rica,
We can travel without a guide,
Just finished massages at the house,
Sitting around the table, talking, laughing, crying,
Wedding scheduled for 4:45,
Getting ready

Day 4 in Costa Rica,
The wedding was marvelous,
The bride and groom were simply beautiful,
On the grounds of the villa it's transformed,
The chef arrives,
The photographer arrives,
It's that time,
The bride is getting dressed,
I help with earrings, dress, shoes,
All is coming along well,
I'm doing a great job as the Matron of Honor,
The ceremony is filled with joy and celebration,
Tears fill the backyard or terrace,
Dinner is lovely and intimate,
Music sounds from my iPhone, a special playlist at the request of
the bride and groom,
Morning breakfast at Luna Azul,
Zip-lining at 1:15,
I'm excited and somewhat nervous at the same time,
We load up on a truck,

Hike to the highest peek,
11 rides,
Ready to quit after ride 1,
An unbelievable experience,
Being thousands of feet in the air,
Have I lost it?
I feel free,
I feel one with the universe,
Everyone is enjoying themselves,
Why did I agree to do this?
Zip-lining.

Day 5,
I wake,
Place feet on carpeted ground,
I sit,
Back aching,
Feels like an elephant has rested on my spine,
I continue to sit taking in the view,
White walls,
Sliding doors not completely closed; the designer let enough room to grasp door from the inside,
The ceiling fans are wooden with 2 blades,
Beige drapery covering the doors,
The glass doors open from one end by grabbing hold of a black handle and sliding the main opening to the right,
The doors remind me of a paper fan,
The entire villa is filled with crafty architecture designs,
On the wall hangs a piece of a tree that resembles an antler head
The land is full of creatures,
Creatures that like to come inside,
Creatures that hop and sing,
Creatures that are green, brown, black, white . . . you name it and they are present, acknowledging our presence on this breathtaking land,
Last night I walked through the house with no shoes on,

An amazing feeling throughout my body was felt,
History suggests the natives were Indians,
I feel the natives,
I see glimpses of them when riding in the truck,
Smaller houses sandwiched between trees,
Doors wide open,
Chairs on the porch,
Native people watching and reading,
I've seen men on horses who wave as we pass in cars,
Kids walking or riding bikes,
Families on motorcycles cruising down the road,
The pace is slower and calmer,
One could get used to this; no hustle and bustle here,
The natives,
The Costa Ricans,
All are beautiful,
The light of the people pour out,
Skin tones vary from smooth caramel to a warm dark chocolate,
I am in awe of the people,
People are not rushing,
People are not texting and driving,
No blowing of horns,
No streetlights,
No one writing a ticket for parking in an unauthorized area,
All the city aspects are void,
There are small villages,
Small villages that house cute markets, boutiques, and restaurants,
Costa Rica reminds me of the south,
Nosara, the name of the small village we visited for zip-lining,
Nicoya, the name of the peninsula we are situated on,
Heaven does exist and I'm enjoying every moment of it,
What an amazing state of mind to be in,
Last evening in Costa Rica,
Had a boat ride to watch turtles, dolphins, and whales,
Hopped on a little boat to get to the bigger boat,
I managed to transfer just fine,

Minutes later the sickness hits my stomach,
I pop several mints to calm my body,
It works on and off,
I pray to God,
I am not sick,
At one point I doze off,
A mom of 2 young children vomits in the sea,
I look at her, she looks at me, and I say, I understand how you feel,
I offer a peppermint to her; she accepts,
There is another couple with 2 small
Children,
The children jump off into the ocean with no hesitation,
The small boat holds 3 families,
We actually saw a few turtles and some dolphins,
Unfortunately no whales due to algae a few days ago,
The view,
The sunset,
All gorgeous,
Upon reaching shore I collect seashells,
We head back and make it back to the villa,
Our last meal is cooked on the grill,
A shrimp curry dish with rice,
Vegetables,
Fruit,
Potatoes,
Delicious,
I didn't touch the beef wrapped in bacon covered with cheese,
We talk around the table,
Do laundry,
And prepare for our last evening in Costa Rica,
I miss my honey.

Turn within

No one around,
I turn to God,
In wanting the physical, I reject it,
I turn to the God that dwells in me,
No one to wipe the tears,
So the tears run freely,
Cleansing all the ill thoughts,
No one around,
Yet I know God is all I need,
I can't make you want me every night,
Although that's my dream,
I am a woman; my purpose in life is to nurture and support,
I don't need much,
I just need all that God has to offer for me in this life,
Feeling your arms around my waist is priceless,
Rubbing you down with oils is memorable,
Listening to you breathe while making love feeds my desire for you,
I will always love you,
Work is your passion,
I can't change that and don't want to,
When I don't hear from you, I know you are knee-deep in your work,
I write to you about how I feel,
Haven't seen you in a week or more,
All that I do for you is how I show my love,
God, help me,
We will always have work to do,
There is more to life than work.

Bookclub

My second invite to discuss my book,
South Shore area,
7 women,
The youngest 50,
Oops, can't forget about me, 29,
A beautiful group,
Read or turn to page 41, happiness, gift, brother, Solomon,
I read a few,
We talked,
Lots of interesting questions and comments,
Are you still with him,
Invite me to the wedding,
Is this book lots of short stories?
How did you come up with the title?
Did you think about other names?
How long did it take you to write this?
How did you find the publishing company?
What inspired you to write?
Does Essence Magazine have your book?
I didn't think your book was all about sex,
Your book reminded me of what it was like to be young,
All this and so much more from 3:30 until 6:30,
Snacking over turkey sandwiches,
Salad and apple pie with ice cream,
Thank you friend,
For opening your home.

Lounging

The sun is beaming,
I lie in bed,
Longer than usual,
Thinking about the day,
Breakfast,
Some fruit,
I make brunch,
My honey enjoys it after church,
We catch up,
Smile,
Kiss,
Talk more,
Laugh,
Nap,
Smile,
I wish he wouldn't leave,
I love loving on him,
Makes me feel better,
I love this man,
December will make 4 years, a lot has happened since we got together,
It's just starting to feel like we are dating since we plunged into
the caring aspect of the relationship,
I always knew we would be together,
At times I wonder,
But I always come back to our love and friendship,
I love loving you.

Sales Guy

At the dealership,
Received several calls about my vehicle being traded in,
Decided against it then reconsidered the offer,
Arrived around 6:45,
Been greeted twice,
Currently waiting on the salesperson's manager to look at the car,
Salesperson is probably fresh out of college,
Yup, he confirms this is a new gig for him,
They keep me waiting,
Why am I here,
Nothings wrong with my 2005 ride,
Curiosity got me here,
Your car is roughly worth $6,000,
Okay, thanks,
Call us,
Now is the time,
Sales folks.

Grandmother Under the Weather Series

It's day 2,
Grandma not feeling too well,
Day 1 was real bad,
Just the day before all was well,
Then she got sick,
Woke up sick,
Went with Grandpa to eat,
Couldn't keep anything down,
Pain in the stomach,
Tried to eat a muffin,
It came back up,
I sit and watch,
Pour you some water,
Place the bin close to you so you don't have to go far to puke,
I sit,
You recline in the chair,
I pray,
I focused on the magnificence of God,
I pray really hard to restore you to your natural self,
You rest,
I watch you sleep,
While watching the cars pass by in LSD,

Day 2,
I pick you and Grandpa up some soup and stop by Walgreens to get
ginger ale and crackers,
You eat an entire bowl of soup as does Andy,
I watch the both of you eat,
You sit by the window,
Grandpa starts to talk,
Not on a subject you want to get into,
He continues with his story,
You let him know that you do not want to hear of this anymore,
I stay silent,
Knowing good and well not to say anything,
The subject is changed but not about anything positive,
Thus continued pattern of negativity cannot be good,
This time I say something,
Darn, I didn't want too,
God, please help our family,
Yes, mistakes have been made but all we have to do is love one
another,
Grandma falls asleep,
I go downstairs,
A few hours pass,
Grandpa knocks on door,
He is afraid,
Grandma is sleeping,
But she hasn't eaten anything,
I remind him that she ate the same portion as you,

Let her rest,
Did she throw up? No.
Come check on her,
I'm afraid to go to sleep,
Okay I will,
I pause,
Feeling the tingling in my dirty hair,
I wash my hair,
Then I visit,
Grandma is snoozing lightly,
We chat and I watch her sleep,
I write now,
Thinking of the pains in my stomach at 5:00 a.m.,
Gas turns to staying on the toilet and not going to work,
The rest I need,
I make breakfast and keep it down,
I love this family,
God keep us in your vision for being.

Advocate

Grandmother is admitted,
Been in pain for a few days,
Checked into the ER,
Searched and examined,
Admitted for the night,
Big bro shows up,
Feels good,
Having the company,
What's most important is that you are here,
I thank you,
Grandma feeling somewhat better,
Will know in the morning which way the doctors will go.
Tuesday, Grandma has surgery,
Gallbladder removed,
Wednesday in hospital,
Thursday home,
Friday resting,
Saturday resting and walking around the house,
Nurse visits,
Says Grandma needs to rest more because blood levels are high,
I put on a pot of beans,
Rice,
Grandma shows me her recipe, sugar,
Salt, crushed peppers.
We make corn bread,
Eat dinner,
Delicious.

No Pity

Things happen,
Maybe for the good,
Maybe for the not-so-good,
Indeed a lesson lies,
A lesson that can be repeated if one doesn't wise up,
I thank God for blessing me with the ability to love and be loved,
There is so much that I want in terms of good health, wealth, and prosperity,
All these things are part of my birthright,
God, help me not to lose myself in anyone or anything,
God, help me to crave you,
God, you are all that I need.

Honda Accord

I woke up today,
Thank you, God,
Work was interesting,
Got an offer about relocating,
Interesting,
Took Grandma to the doctor's office,
All is well,
Stitches are invisible,
No restrictions on diet,
Drink more fluids,
Walk,
Walk,
As much as you can,
Back to the car we go,
Arrive home,
Heat some fish, rice, and salad.
I look at the calendar,
Today is the last day of the Honda sale,
I'm gonna do it!
Trade it in,
It has been 7 years,
My first car,
Ready for something a little bigger,
Thinking about hitting the road,
Don't want to worry about tires, engine, or anything else,
I'm sitting in the dealership,
Arrived at 7:30 p.m.,
Doing paperwork now,
Reading my book *The Power of Now* by Eckhart Tolle,
Waiting on my car to arrive,
I'm excited,
This is indeed an early birthday gift,
Happy 30th, Gloria.

Another Day

Stop by the dealership,
Pick up papers from school,
Make it to center by 10:30,
Let intern know we can do lunch at 11:45,
A coworker ask for a ride to Jewel,
Nice ride in my new ride,
Make it back to center,
Work on evaluation for intern at King,
It's time for lunch,
We load up in car,
Not before intern moves my car because someone parks so close
that I cannot get in,
Off we go,
Driving through the city,
Showing where I grew up,
Where my mom worked,
The dynamics of living and growing up in this area,
Loving this day,
The buffet at Home Run Inn is tasty,
People are all over,
Babies are conversing in baby talk,
We talk,
And talk,
Lessons learned,
Challenges,
Make it back to center,
No one is looking for us,
Back to my work area the back activity room,
I text my honey,
We haven't seen much of each other lately,
We text,
You are in a meeting,

Time goes by you call,
I step outside,
There is a calmness we have,
We speak,
From the heart,
Not afraid of answers,
We will always be friends,
Yes, things have changed,
What's next,
I want to be near you,
That doesn't happen,
Need to shop for dinner,
Call Aunt for kale recipe,
No dinner cooking tonight,
Grandma has prepared dinner,
Granndpa worries about her cooking,
Docs wants her to take it easy,
We chat for a while,
I went downstairs and unpack groceries,
Wash up,
Clean the tub,
Eat salad and beans,
You say you will call,
You don't.

Peoria Packaging Butcher Shop

It's Sunday,
I'm up,
Feeling good,
Make Grandma oatmeal and croissants for myself,
Headed west,
Taking Aunt to Butcher shop,
Not much traffic,
People are slowly rolling along Ashland, Halsted and Ogden Street too.
I arrive in my old neighborhood.